The Elusive Sentence

The Elusive Sentence

Recovering the Rudiments of Writing

Rita Eulalie Hatfield and
Leta Marie Young

ROWMAN & LITTLEFIELD
Lanham • Boulder • New York • London

Published by Rowman & Littlefield
A wholly owned subsidiary of The Rowman & Littlefield Publishing Group, Inc.
4501 Forbes Boulevard, Suite 200, Lanham, Maryland 20706
www.rowman.com

Unit A, Whitacre Mews, 26-34 Stannary Street, London SE11 4AB

Copyright © 2016 by Rita Eulalie Hatfield and Leta Marie Young

All rights reserved. No part of this book may be reproduced in any form or by any electronic or mechanical means, including information storage and retrieval systems, without written permission from the publisher, except by a reviewer who may quote passages in a review.

British Library Cataloguing in Publication Information Available

Library of Congress Cataloging-in-Publication Data Available

ISBN: 978-1-4758-2338-7 (cloth : alk. paper)
ISBN: 978-1-4758-2339-4 (pbk. : alk. paper)
ISBN: 978-1-4758-2340-0 (electronic)

∞™ The paper used in this publication meets the minimum requirements of American National Standard for Information Sciences—Permanence of Paper for Printed Library Materials, ANSI/NISO Z39.48-1992.

Printed in the United States of America

We dedicate this work in loving memory of our parents.
Our mother, Catherine M. Puri, PhD, was a nurse, educator, and scholar.
She was extremely successful, accomplished, and intelligent.
She developed the nursing program at Oregon Institute of
Technology in Klamath Falls, Oregon, and retired as the CEO
of the California State Board of Nursing.
She was extraordinarily capable, nurturing, and compassionate.
She passed to us her love of learning, her passion for education,
and her enthusiasm to aspire to make a difference, and she
gave us the confidence to reach for the stars.

Our father, Bard F. Hendricks, was our teacher.
He taught us guitar, singing, yodeling, song writing, poetry,
art, dancing, tumbling, diving, horsemanship, archery, and
how to play a myriad of games.
He was a "Mary Poppins Dad."
He instilled in us a responsibility to befriend and defend the underdog.
He taught us that every person matters and has something
worthwhile to offer.
He passed to us his love for children and inspired our teaching style.
He showed us that the most memorable and engaging lessons
are those that are creative, active, and fun.

Contents

Preface — xi
Acknowledgments — xiii
Introduction — xv

Part I: Language Objective: Sentence-Level Writing Intervention — 1

Why should we teach sentence-level writing? — 1

  1 The Problem: Inverted Writing Pedagogy — 3

  2 The Solution: Sentence-Level Writing — 7

  3 Sentence-Level Writing Intervention — 11
      Elementary Writing Pedagogy — 12

  4 Linguistic & Musical Syntax — 17
      Audiation Theory for Music and Writing — 18

How do we teach sentence-level writing? — 23

  5 Ingham-Webster-Pudewa Method — 25
      Dress-Ups — 25
      Scaffolding Common Core State Standards for Writing — 38

6	Writers: Middle School, High School, College, and Beyond	41
	Advanced Stylistic Techniques	43
7	Sheltered Instruction for Writing	47

Part II: Content Objective: Cognitively Differentiated Learning — 49

What is cognitively differentiated learning? — 49

8	Cognitively Differentiated Learning	51

Why should we teach academic content through arts-integrated experiences? — 55

9	Rationale: Teaching through the Arts	57
	Art and Cognition	58
10	Arts-Integrated Learning	61
	Rehearsal Effect	62
	Elaboration Effect	63
	Generation Effect	64
	Enactment Effect	65
	Production Effect	66
	Effort After Meaning Effect	67
	Emotional Arousal Effect	67
	Picture Superiority Effect	68
11	Arts-Integrated Instruction and Cognition	71
	Writing: Cognitive and Physical Skills	73
	Cognitively Differentiated Teaching and Learning	75

Why should we teach academic content through song? — 79

12	Song as a Teaching Tool	81
	Balanced Learning through Horizontal Differentiation	83
13	Operational Definitions	87
	Rationale: Teaching Content through Song	88

14 Inherited Dissociated Philosophy	91
Historical Background of Mnemonic Learning	94
15 Neuroscience of Music and Memory	97
Memory and Music	98
Music and Mnemonics	99
Mnemonics and Diverse Learners	100
Assumptions and Final Thoughts on Mnemonic Song	101
16 Method and Practice: Putting It All Together	103
Sample Weekly Outline	105
17 Best Practice for Writing Instruction	111
18 Training Teachers for the New Millennium	115
Hippocratic Oath for Educators	118
19 Final Reflection	121
Appendix A: Arts-Integrated Resources	125
Appendix B: Writing Matrix	129
Appendix C: Composition Checksheet	131
Appendix D: Sample Syllabus	133
Appendix E: Webster's Formulas and Chants for Written Communication	141
References	145

Preface

Across our nation, many within the educational system complain that America's children do not write well. Most teachers recognize a problem, yet struggle to provide a solution. Hatfield and Young assert that a solution has been proposed, but it has been slow to permeate the public school system. They posit that the missing piece from most elementary writing curricula is rudimentary instruction at the sentence level.

Studies indicate that students cannot write well because they do not know basic parts of speech, and they are missing a crucial understanding of how language works (Tyre, 2012). The authors' language objectives are the following: to reintroduce a method for teaching the structure and style of sentence construction; to rediscover an explicit concrete visual approach for teaching the various elements found in great sentences; to reexamine various ways that kernels (simple sentences), phrases, and clauses may combine to create a variety of sentence openers; and to rethink our pedagogy for elementary writing.

To practice this method, students need something to write about. Hatfield and Young use grade-level content from social science and science. Like sheltered instruction, this writing intervention has dual objectives: one for language and one for content. In this writing model, content objectives are supported through a variety of cognitively differentiated activities that help cement content learning into students' long-term memory. This model encompasses a pedagogy that strives to accommodate for the neurodiversity of young learners by delivering content through multiple pathways of learning.

This writing intervention is the missing instructional piece for writing skills acquisition—the foundational framework that helps teachers, students, parents, and writers of all ages to understand how to craft well-written sentences and paragraphs. This writing method presents educators a phenomenal tool that will inspire the confidence needed to teach writing. It offers students clearly defined outlines and rubrics for what success looks like and it provides a writing model that facilitates memory for other content objectives required by the state.

Acknowledgments

With deepest gratitude we thank the following professionals for assisting us with peer reviews:

Sheryl J. Reinisch, EdD
Dean, College of Education
Concordia University
Portland, Oregon

Trish Lichau Shields, PhD
Vice President, Educational
    Delivery Systems
Concordia University
Portland, Oregon

Paul E. Dennison, PhD
President, Edu-Kinesthetics
Ventura, California

Carol Buckwald, MEd
Reading Specialist
Retired

David B. Hatfield, BS, RT (R)

Jane Koivisto, MSEd
Reading Specialist
Professor Emeritus
Concordia University
Portland, Oregon

Jen Sah-Loeung, MAT
TESOL Certificate
Intercultural Communication and
    Children at Risk

Mariale M. Hardiman, EdD
Dean
John Hopkins University School of
    Education
Baltimore, Maryland

Eve Connell, MA, TESOL
Writer/Editor/Communications
    Consultant
Undergraduate/Graduate Professor
Oregon and California

Introduction

> Executive Mansion
>
> Washington, Nov 21, 1864
>
> To Mrs. Bisby, Boston, Mass,
>
> Dear Madam,
>
> I have been shown in the files of the War Department a statement of the Adjutant General of Massachusetts that you are the mother of five sons who have died gloriously on the field of battle. I feel how weak and fruitless must be any word of mine which should attempt to beguile you from the grief of a loss so overwhelming. But I cannot refrain from tendering you the consolation that may be found in the thanks of the republic they died to save. I pray that our Heavenly Father may assuage the anguish of your bereavement, and leave you only the cherished memory of the loved and lost, and the solemn pride that must be yours to have laid so costly a sacrifice upon the altar of freedom.
>
> Yours very sincerely and respectfully,
> A. Lincoln

Have you ever wondered how a home-schooled backwoodsman, who had no formal education, could compose prized literary documents, such as the Gettysburg Address and this letter that hangs on the wall of Brasenose College, Oxford University, in England? This letter is on display because it is considered a "model of purest English, rarely, if ever, surpassed" (Cook, 1958, p. 174). What exquisitely written expressions of sympathy Abraham Lincoln composed in his correspondence to a mother who had lost five sons in the Civil War! Using just four sentences, President Lincoln conveyed profound sentiment with incredibly articulate, succinct, yet elegant structure and style.

How was it that this informally educated U.S. president, as well as other early Americans, could articulate their thoughts so masterfully? It is safe to assume that people were not any smarter back then than they are today, so why could some in that era, who were considered poorly educated by modern standards, write so well? What has changed from yesteryear to today?

Across the breadth of our nation, many within our educational system complain that America's children do not write well (Cavanagh, 2003; Jones, 1995; Schmoker, 2006). These critics identify a problem, yet few propose a solution. Some discern there is a problem at the foundational level of our writing pedagogy—that there is a missing piece (Tyre, 2012). A solution exists, but it has been slow to permeate the corridors of the public school system in America. Some propose that the missing link in most elementary writing curricula is rudimentary instruction at the sentence level. We agree.

Peg Tyre, director of strategy at the Edwin Gould Foundation and author of *The Good School: How Smart Parents Get Their Kids the Education They Deserve* (2011), also agrees. She writes in her article "The Writing Revolution" (2012), published in a special edition of *The Atlantic* called "Special Report: New Ideas for Schools," that:

> Fifty years ago, elementary-school teachers taught the general rules of spelling and the structure of sentences. Later instruction focused on building solid paragraphs into full-blown essays. Some kids mastered it, but many did not. About 25 years ago, in an effort to enliven instruction and get more kids writing, schools of education began promoting a different approach. The popular thinking was that writing should be *"caught, not taught"* explains Stephen Graham, a professor of education instruction at Arizona State University. Roughly, it was supposed to work like this: Give students interesting creative-writing assignments; put that writing in a fun, social context in which kids share their work. Kids, the theory goes, will "catch" what they need in order to be successful writers. Formal lessons in grammar, sentence structure, and essay-writing took a back seat to creative expression. (Tyre, 2012, pp. 99–100)

Tyre (2012) also relates Principal Deidre DeAngelis's challenge to rescue her failing high school, New Dorp on Staten Island. After a detailed investigation, "the principal and her staff came up with a singular answer: bad writing" (p. 97). Their findings indicated that their students could not write well because they lacked rudimentary speech and language skills. They observed, "Consistently, one of the largest differences between failing and successful students was that only the latter could express their thoughts on the page" (p. 97).

If we want to scaffold successful student writers, some feel it would be helpful if we gave them a formula for what successful sentences and paragraphs look like. Tyre (2012) interviewed and quoted Judith Hochman, author of the successful Hochman Program for writing and former head of the Windward School in New York, who stated:

> The thing is, kids *need* a formula, at least at first, because what we are asking them to do is very difficult. So, let's stop acting like they should just know how to do it. Give them a formula! Later, when they understand the rules of good writing, they can figure out how to break them. (Tyre, 2012, p. 100)

Lucy Calkins, a professor at Columbia University's Teachers College, disagrees with Hochman and argues that formulaic instruction will cause some students to tune out. Calkins believes, "Kids need to see their work reach other readers. . . . They need to have choices in the questions they write about, and a way to find their voice" (Tyre, 2012, p. 101). We argue, "Why are we not offering students both—a concrete visual for the elements we expect to see in their writing, and choices for how they express their voice within a social context?"

The principal of New Dorp High School determined to change one thing: to singularly focus on systematically teaching the skills and techniques that underlie successful analytic writing. The results were extraordinary. Tyre (2012) reported, "New Dorp, once the black sheep of the borough, is being held up as a model of successful school turnaround" (p. 97). The pedagogical pendulum for writing standards is starting to swing away from self-expression to favoring systematic instruction that teaches thoughtful, coherent communication. For those states aligned with Common Core State Standards, elementary students are expected to write informative, expository, and persuasive essays, not just in English class but in history and science classes as well.

Part I of our study describes the language objective for this writing method. We introduce a sentence-level writing intervention and provide teachers and students instructional fundamentals for explicitly teaching the structure and style of composing a variety of interesting sentences and paragraphs. After observing a successful systematic writing program, Tyre (2012) suggests, "perhaps certain instructional fundamentals—fundamentals that schools have devalued or forgotten—need to be rediscovered, updated, and reintroduced" (p. 101).

Tyre (2012) succinctly sums up the impetus behind our work. Our desire is to *reintroduce* a method for teaching writing that was introduced to us by a remarkable first grade teacher from Saskatchewan, Canada, and to *rediscover* a treasure that should be taught in every classroom across America. After exploring studies in neuroscience regarding the relationship between linguistic and musical syntax, we also want to *update* our pedagogical thinking about the way that we approach writing instruction (Li & Brand, 2010; Patel, 2003).

In Part II, we switch our focus to the content objectives for this writing intervention. We investigate studies within neuroscience and cognitive psychology to provide a rationale for modifying today's pedagogical practice for teaching the content objectives based on the way the brain learns. We introduce a cognitively differentiated approach to writing that integrates academics from other content areas and supports learning through a variety of multisensory activities.

We demonstrate how cognitively differentiated instruction is naturally embedded in this sentence-level writing intervention. From neuroscience, we learn how art-integrated activities affect the learning and remembering processes in the brain. We also demonstrate how a cognitively differentiated writing model may be integrated across multiple academic domains and may be fully multisensory, while explicitly teaching a variety of sentence structure and style conventions.

This writing intervention provides an expedient opportunity to integrate across the curriculum and teach grade-level content for social science, science, and art. To practice this method for teaching sentence construction, children need something to write about. This system provides an excellent vehicle for integrating the academic subjects from the Common Core State Standards that so often get overlooked with today's emphasis on literacy and math.

Throughout this study we introduce the application of a sentence-level writing intervention and we update our writing pedagogy. We also restructure the writing workshop to intentionally integrate multiple disciplines and we cognitively differentiate for multiple ways of knowing and learning. Using cognitively differentiated activities as a teaching methodology throughout curricula, we strive to accommodate for the neurodiversity of learners and deliver academic content via the multiple languages of learning (Parsons, 1992), characterized by the learning modalities whereby one understands, perceives, and learns the best.

This sentence-level writing intervention is the missing instructional piece for writing skills acquisition—the foundational framework that helps teachers, students, parents, and writers of all ages to understand how to craft well-written sentences. We believe if we give teachers and students a roadmap for what successful writing looks like, and if we restore the proper pedagogy for writing instruction, then we can produce a caliber of writers equivalent in eloquence to America's most renowned authors—Mark Twain, John Steinbeck, Abraham Lincoln, and others.

1

LANGUAGE OBJECTIVE

Sentence-Level Writing Intervention

Why should we teach sentence-level writing?

quality adjective

strong verb

"ly" word

Sentence Opener

who/which clause

adverb clause

vss

Dress-Ups

subject

prepositional phrase

1

The Problem
Inverted Writing Pedagogy

When we think about the natural development of writing skills, the progression of complexity moves sequentially from writing the letters of the alphabet, to words, to sentences, to paragraphs, and then to stories. Then we introduce the functions of writing, the writing process (prewriting, drafting, revising, editing, and publication), and the principles of writing assessment (the six traits: ideas and content, organization, voice, word choice, sentence fluency, and conventions) (Culham, 2005). In kindergarten, students first learn to write the alphabet letters, and then to decode and write words. Toward the middle of kindergarten, students are taught to write a simple sentence such as, "I like my dog."

The problem is that after students are able to string together a basic subject-verb-object sentence, further instruction in the art of crafting sentences is seldom seen. Instead of focusing on writing instruction at the sentence level during the early elementary years, we jump forward to teaching the functions, process, and principles of writing assessment. Our writing pedagogy feels inverted and unnatural.

Imagine a piano student coming to his very first lesson. The piano teacher pulls out a big chart and begins to explain the six principles (traits) of music that are found in the work of great musicians. The following analogy portrays the scene:

> The novice smiles. He sits wide-eyed, feet dangling in midair, eyes eager with anticipation, hands shaking from nervousness, worried whether this will be fun, yet curious to discover the mystery of the keys, especially the black ones, because black is his favorite color. The teacher points to the chart. Six principles are listed. The teacher's voice reverberates with authority, and her words surge and ebb as she lectures.

Music expresses ideas and content. One should play in a way that expresses clear, focused ideas, and content should be interesting and engaging. Music is organized into measures, phrases, and stanzas, and it must communicate the appropriate voice to the audience. Note choice is intended to convey a message in an exceptionally interesting, precise, yet natural way that is appropriate to the purpose intended. Phrasing must be fluent, and one's playing should have flow and rhythm. Phrases should show a high degree of craftsmanship, with consistently strong and varied structure that makes listening easy and enjoyable. Lastly, the best music should demonstrate exceptionally strong conventions, as in tempo, meter, dynamics, and syntax.

The teacher pauses. She looks satisfied. She puts music before her pupil, and she asks him to play. The pupil stares at the sheet music before him; the teacher's words were obviously words he understood, but they made no sense to him. He feels lost, bewildered, unprepared, and he's embarrassed. He feels stupid; he does not know how to begin. He sighs, his shoulders sag down, his head falls forward, and his face turns red. The novice cries.

A music educator would not dream of taking this instructional approach when teaching a first-year music student, yet in many instances teachers are asked to use a similar approach to teach children elementary writing. Children do not have complex language patterns such as diverse syntactical phrases or varieties of sentence openers automatically stored in their brains, any more than a first-year piano student has note pattern recognition and interesting musical phrases automatically stored in his. These are learned through modeling and extensive guided practice, one phrase at a time, starting with the simple and then moving to the more complex. If writing were taught using the same methods used for teaching music, dance, art, gymnastics, or any other creative art form, then students would learn to write.

Creative arts pedagogy demands an explicit, systematic, and sequential approach. To be effective, one cannot skip steps and expect satisfactory results. In writing, without ample practice at the sentence level, one cannot expect proficient skill at the paragraph level and beyond. In music, learners practice musical phrases involving one note before they play phrases using parts of chords. Students practice songs playing one note with each hand before they play songs involving parts of a chord with both hands. The progression of skills acquisition proceeds sequentially and systematically. Creative arts pedagogy instructs incrementally, provides ample opportunities for guided practice, and generally requires liberal amounts of independent practice to attain proficiency.

The problem is we have been applying the wrong pedagogy to writing instruction. Like the analogy of the novice piano student, we have not been teaching incrementally and systematically and, inadvertently, we have skipped an essential rudimentary step—teaching the elementary foundations of sentence and paragraph construction.

If students have not practiced writing with a variety of forms, phrases, and clauses, then how can we expect them to know what these elements are? If they have not experimented with the various ways these elements can be creatively arranged and assembled to produce a variety of sentence openers, then how can we expect them to open their sentences with anything other than "I" or "The"? If they do not have a lexicon of phrasing patterns in their minds to work with, then how can we expect students to generate reliably correct and sophisticated language patterns in their writing? (Pudewa, 2004). If we have an expectation for what elements we would like to see in our students' writing, then we should define the expectation and provide plenty of opportunities for modeling and guided practice.

2

The Solution

Sentence-Level Writing

To build a firm foundation for writing skills acquisition, it is paramount that we do not leave out the underpinnings that scaffold and support the whole structure. If we want students to produce more than a subject-verb-object sentence, then we must teach what that looks like.

The framework for teaching this sentence-level intervention is based on the *Blended Sight-Sound Program of Learning* (2004) as taught by Anna Ingham, the text *Blended Structure and Style in Composition* (1994) by James B. Webster, professor emeritus, Dalhousie University, Halifax, Nova Scotia, and the seminar *Teaching Writing: Structure and Style* (2015) by Andrew Pudewa.

When we first started teaching, we both felt fairly confident that we could competently teach most subjects—with the sole exception of writing. How to teach writing successfully was elusive, and we were perplexed as to how to begin. Although we considered ourselves reasonably accomplished writers, we did not know how to explain and define for our students what good writing looked like. We could explain to our students what was wrong with what they wrote, but we could not define for them what they should do in the first place to write well.

We felt incredibly insecure and inadequate with this subject matter and resorted to what most curricula offered; we put a blank piece of paper in front of our students, gave them a writing prompt, and asked them to write. Then we would correct their sentences with them, pointing out the elements that were wrong. It felt like such an ineffective strategy, but we were helpless as to how to provide our students more concrete guidance.

In the early 1990s, our public school charter brought to Alaska *The Institute for Excellence in Writing*. Pudewa's (2015) writing method was based on the work of Dr. James B. Webster (1994), a university professor of history. Shortly after he began teaching in the university setting, Webster found himself frustrated because his students could not turn out acceptable college papers.

One day he was visiting his aunt, Anna Ingham, a first grade teacher. He picked up some of her students' writing samples that were lying on the coffee table. He noticed that Aunt Anna's first grade class could produce writing with better structure and style than most of his university students. Dr. Webster (1994) asked his aunt to share her writing methods, and from this, he created his *Blended Structure and Style in Composition,* a writing intervention for his university students.

Soon the word on campus was that if you wanted to learn how to write, you should take Dr. Webster's history class. In 1995, Anna Ingham received Canada's second highest civilian honor, Member of the Order of Canada, in recognition of her educational contributions, which have enriched the lives of children and her contemporaries (Ingham, 2004).

Andrew Pudewa took Webster's (1994) work and created an elementary through high school curriculum for the *Blended Sight-Sound Approach.* Through Pudewa's (2015) seminar we were introduced to the Ingham-Webster-Pudewa method for writing, and for both of us, the experience was novel and momentous. Pudewa (2015) explicitly defined how to teach a child to write sentences with a variety of structure and style. Exposure to a systematic method for teaching writing evoked in us a refreshing sense of relief, because now we had concrete curriculum in our hands that explained the craft of writing.

While earning her master's degree, Eulalie heard a seasoned middle school teacher say, "I do not like to teach writing because I really do not know how." She felt such empathy for her because she remembered how frustrating it was to not feel adequately equipped to teach something that she wanted to teach well. The Ingham-Webster-Pudewa (2015) approach demystified the elusive foundations of writing instruction. It laid the instructional cornerstone with clarity and precision. It is a sentence-level writing intervention that plainly and simply teaches the mechanics of sentence construction.

In the 1960s, in the field of special education, a similar sentence intervention called *sentence combining* was introduced and used with positive results (Saddler & Asaro-Saddler, 2010). With sentence combining, the teacher would create several kernel sentences, provide in parenthesis various conjunctions and clauses, and then ask students to combine the kernel sentences with the suggested conjunctions or clauses to create complex sentences.

While this method demonstrated how sentences are arrangements of kernel sentences, phrases, and clauses, sentence combining is a teacher-generated activity, whereas the Ingham-Webster-Pudewa (2015) method is a student-generated activity. Students need to learn how to write within a real-world context and from content that they are studying. Rather than providing students teacher-generated kernels and clauses, a more effective strategy is to have the students brainstorm their own propositions (short summary statements), phrases, and clauses from informational text about topics that they need to study and know and are interested in.

As educators, our dearest desire is to help teachers and students feel confident with teaching and learning writing. We firmly believe we need to give students outlines and rubrics for what success looks like before we ask them to write. We introduce the sentence-level portion of the Ingham-Webster-Pudewa (2015) method, but this only skims the surface of what is offered through their systematic writing curriculum. We hope that this presentation of the rudimentary part of their method evokes a deeper study into this effective approach to writing instruction.

We encourage public schools across America to invite *The Institute for Excellence for Writing* into their schools. Pudewa (2015) and his team of specialists have been teaching students, parents, and educators for over twenty years. As a skilled Toastmaster, Pudewa (2015) articulately presents the Ingham-Webster-Pudewa writing method for K–12. His seminar, *Teaching Writing: Structure and Style,* provides students and educators a solid foundation in the skills listed in table 2.1.

Table 2.1. Teaching Writing: Structure and Style

Note making and outlines	Writing from notes	Retelling narrative stories
Summarizing a reference	Writing from pictures	Summarizing multiple references
Inventive writing	Formal essay models	Formal critique
Writing about literature	Stylistic techniques	

(Pudewa, 2015, p. 1)

The new writing standards require K–12 students to write in several genres (persuasive, expository, narrative, descriptive, opinion/critique, and report/essay), and to write in every class, not just English class. Comprehensive systems for teaching these writing skills are rare. Clearly, no single program will ever incorporate everything there is to learn about writing. Pudewa's *Teaching Writing: Structure and Style,* however, when followed consistently, will prepare students to meet the challenges of the new writing standards.

We believe there is a solution to the problem of why America's children struggle to effectively communicate their thoughts in writing. After we were exposed to the Ingham-Webster-Pudewa (2015) method, it became evident that we were missing a vital piece of instruction—a foundational part that we were never taught. Instead of continuing on a course where we expect students to know what they have not been taught, let's change our pedagogy, and explicitly teach them which elements should be found in their writing before we ask them to write.

Let us offer students outlines and rubrics for what success looks like, model what success looks like, and systematically teach them to be successful writers. For us, learning the mechanics of sentence and paragraph construction provided a primer for writing instruction. It clearly defined for us how to begin. Possessing a precise pragmatic method evoked confidence and generated an enthusiasm for teaching elementary writing. Now, we feel properly equipped with the necessary tools to help students succeed and we are confident we can effectively teach the art and craft of writing. We want all teachers to feel similarly equipped and confident, to know they have in their hands the tools that demystify the elusive sentence.

3

Sentence-Level Writing Intervention

Song of Hope
There's a rainbow in every teardrop you're crying
There's a love song in every treetop above
There's a star's face in every snowflake that's falling
There's hope when we reach out in love
There's a diamond in every dewdrop that glistens
There's a goldmine in every sunset you see
There's a rainbow in every teardrop you're crying
So dry up your tears and believe (repeat)

—Adapted from a song by Slim Whitman and Erwin King

Words communicate thoughts. Sentences communicate ideas. Skillfully constructed sentences may creatively express words so eloquently, it could be said that composing a great sentence is like choreographing a waltz with words.

Sentences are the most important building blocks of written communication. They combine ideas into complex expressions of thought, conveying information through a series of kernal sentences, phrases, and clauses, which may be cleverly arranged and manipulated to create an interesting variety of syntactical structure and style. An understanding of how sentences combine is foundational to learning to write well. Learning syntactical strategies through explicit sentence-level instruction is the basis of writing skills acquisition. Our intervention defines the strategies that elementary students may use in their writing to ensure that their sentences will be effective, sophisticated—and possibly even elegant.

This writing method is a sentence-level writing intervention, because the language objective is direct, systematic instruction in the mechanics of sentence construction. This intervention is integrated because it disseminates instruction across the following domains:

- **Writing Instruction:** A sentence-level writing intervention to be used in conjunction with existing writing curricula
- **Multiple Disciplines:** Language arts, social science, science, and the creative arts integrated to support the sentence-level writing objectives and grade-level content objectives
- **Cognitively Differentiated Instruction:** Academic content delivered through multiple symbol processing systems or the various languages of learning (Parsons, 1992)

This writing model is cognitively differentiated because the pedagogical methods take into consideration neuroeducational research on how students think and learn (Ginns, 2005; Johansson, 2008; Rinne, Gregory, Yarmolinskaya, & Hardiman, 2011). The method prescribed in this model is a culmination of the following factors: gleanings from the expertise of master educators, years of teaching experience, a lifelong passion for educational pedagogy, and a fascination for how the brain learns. It results from our evolution as right-brain, creative/intuitive educators and learners.

We concede that there seems to be cause for educators' complaints about writing instruction (Cavanagh, 2003; Schmoker, 2006; Tyre, 2012). The purpose of our book is to propose solutions and rationales based on scientific research and *best practice*. We believe the problem begins with our pedagogy for writing. Perhaps we should reconsider how we have approached writing, review where we have been, and rethink our pedagogy for writing skills acquisition.

ELEMENTARY WRITING PEDAGOGY

We know that learning theories lend themselves more appropriately to specific stages of child development, and to specific academic subject areas. Vygotsky (1934b, 1986), a renowned educational psychologist, quotes Franz Brentano regarding the development of learning theories:

> There are many psychologies, but there is no one unified psychology. We may add that there are so many psychologies precisely because there is no one psychology. As long as we lack a generally accepted system incorporating all available psychological knowledge, any important factual discovery inevitably leads to the creation of a new theory to fit the newly observed facts. (Vygotsky, 1934b, 1986, p. 13)

Precisely because the facts we choose to consider vary, factors such as cultural influences differ (Vygotsky, 1929), environmental influences vary (Vygotsky, 1934a), cognitive developmental needs change (Huitt & Hummel, 2003), and inevitably, because educational objectives vary, this means the theory, application, and approaches must vary.

For instance, during Piaget's sensorimotor and preoperational stages, discovery learning (Bruner, 1961; Dewey, 1902; Piaget, 1969) is a very appropriate approach. This is a time when children are exploring their world. Every day holds new discoveries. Babies and toddlers rapidly gain acquisition of new knowledge and skills, and it is a time of expansive mental, motor, and linguistic growth.

Math and science also lend themselves to inquiry-based learning. Teachers may plan projects that experientially lead students to discover and begin to understand some of the universal laws and principles that explain their physical world. However, once students can reason, read, relate, and write, some learning is more effective when instruction is more directed and structured—certainly when it challenges and scaffolds student learning within their zone of proximal development (Kim, 2001). Certain subjects lend themselves to a social constructivist approach—the "I do, we do, you do" approach using a gradual release of responsibility.

Vygotsky's social constructivist theory and model is connected with experiential learning within a social context and builds on Piaget's epistemological theory of constructivism. Vygotsky's "gradual release of responsibility" (GRR) model is a teaching approach that progressively releases responsibility for learning from the teacher to the student. One element crucial to the GRR model is the idea of "instructional scaffolding," which means teachers and peers support or "scaffold" student learning until the student is able to work independently.

Vygotsky also purported that teachers and peers should scaffold learning within a person's "zone of proximal development," which is the difference between what a student can do with assistance and what he or she can do without help. Hence the phrases "I do" (teacher models), "we do" (guided practice, shared work, partner work), and "you do" (independent work). Vygotsky's social constructivist model is deeply embedded in *best practice* (Zemelman, Daniels, & Hyde, 2005) and is documented as an effective approach for a diverse population of learners (Kong & Peterson, 2003).

The whole-language approach (e.g., look at the word shape—if we immerse students in rich language experiences, then children will naturally learn to read), which was based on a discovery learning approach to reading, was not very successful. According to two large-scale studies, one by the United Research Council's Commission on Preventing Reading Difficulties in Young Children (Griffen, Snow, & Burns, 1998) and the other by the United States National

Reading Panel (2000), reading specialists determined that five elements are essential to reading instruction: explicit systematic phonics instruction, phonological awareness, reading comprehension, vocabulary, and fluency.

Whole language was founded on the false assumption that, just as children naturally learned to speak, so too will they naturally learn to read. In an explanation on brain plasticity, Johansson (2008) stated:

> That one effortlessly learns to talk and to sing while being exposed to language and music is an example of developmental plasticity. . . . In contrast, reading, writing, and playing an instrument are cultural innovations that require specific training, and that involves training/learning-induced plasticity. (p. 415)

If people were naturally capable of learning to read and write, would we see indigenous peoples with oral-based cultures or societies with high rates of illiteracy? Most educators agree that reading and writing require a teacher-directed approach, one that involves training, modeling, and lots of guided practice. Reading specialists have determined that most children require direct instruction in phonics and vocabulary, and they need extensive practice to develop fluency and comprehension skills (Adams & Bruck, 1995, p. 15).

Many people have felt that over the past half century writing instruction has been more like a giant experiment in discovery. Most of us were taught some generalities of sentence construction, such as that a sentence begins with a capital letter and ends with some form of punctuation. We learned that the subject contained the noun and the predicate, the verb. Beyond that, it was left up to us to discover what great writing looked like. Our instructor was the teacher's "red ink pen," which edited all our mistakes. Donald Graves, a professor emeritus from the University of New Hampshire, confessed, "At one point I realized I didn't teach writing, I corrected" (Jones, 1995, p. 63).

America's approach to writing instruction has failed miserably. In an article in *Education Weekly* (2003), Cavanagh reports that the University of Oregon unveiled the results of a two-year study called *Understanding University Success*. In the report Professor Albert R. Matheny speaks of his experience as the director of academic advising:

> Even as the pool of freshmen seemed to get better every year, many of those 6,500 or so entrants had no idea how to turn out a college-level paper Mr. Matheny said. They all have 3.8 GPAs and 1300s on their SATs. They're the students who should be the cream of the crop, but we find that they can't write. (Cavanagh, 2003, p. 6)

Discovery learning is not an effective strategy when it comes to teaching reading or writing. Educators have approached writing like they would a science, but writing is a creative activity. They have mistakenly believed that an early introduction to the principles of assessment and the process of writing is sufficient for instruction, yet it is obvious that this approach is not working.

We believe that writing is not a science, that it requires a different pedagogy. Grammar is a science, but writing demands explicit, systematic, sequential instruction coupled with lots of guided practice—it requires a social constructivist approach to learning, as do most creative endeavors.

We have heard teachers say, "All we need to do is teach students to read, and then they will naturally learn to write—that good readers will make good writers." To use a similar analogy, this would be like telling violin students that if they just listened to the recordings of violin virtuosos they would learn to play well. This approach is missing its most vital element: to play well, you have to see playing modeled, and then you must put in many grueling hours of practice.

Reading well is not equivalent to writing well. In comparison, reading is a somewhat passive activity. When we read, we read for content; normally, we do not pay much attention to forms and syntax of sentence construction (Adams & Bruck, 1995, p. 11). Most good readers read fast. One can gloss over words and still glean content, story, and main ideas.

Having the ability to read complex material does not guarantee that one can write complex written language patterns with coherent meaning any more than watching superstar basketball players on television will make one a great ball player. Writing is an active endeavor, one that requires lots of practice to perform well. Like learning to play the violin or basketball, the more you practice the more proficient your performance.

Perhaps we have been applying the wrong pedagogy for writing, and consequently have put the cart before the horse. Instead of first focusing on sentence-level forms, phrases, clauses, and stylistic techniques of syntactical structure—the method, craft, and practice of constructing sentences—we jump straight to the principles and the process. Peregoy and Boyle (2008) cite a 2005 Paul Gruwell cartoon depicting a teacher standing in front of a student sitting at his desk. The student has thrown up his hands in exasperation and said, "I can't REvise; I ain't even VISED yet!" (Peregoy & Boyle, 2008, p. 241). How can students edit and revise their compositions when they are not given a model of what "better or revised" looks like? Students are left to shoot in the dark and are forced to play the writing game, "Guess My Expectation!"

When Benjamin Franklin was a boy, one of seventeen children, his father could not afford to send him to school; therefore, his formal schooling ended at the age of ten. Franklin was determined not to be stuck working in his father's candle shop, so he read and studied voraciously to pursue his dream of becoming a writer. Carefully studying syntax and practicing writing the words of successful authors, he taught himself how to write.

When he was twelve, Franklin's brother, James, apprenticed him to work in his printing shop. By age fifteen, Franklin asked if he could submit a letter for publication in his brother's paper, *The New England Courant,* but James denied his request. Using a pseudonym, "Mrs. Silence Dogood," Franklin began submitting letters, which launched his famous career as an author.

Benjamin Franklin challenged himself by studying compositions beyond his zone of proximal development. Copying great sentences and passages of accomplished authors, he practiced until he could compose his own original sentences. The lesson that educators can glean from his life is that learning to write requires a deliberate systematic study at the sentence level. If we teach children the explicitly defined structural elements of writing, then, like Franklin, they will begin to build a lexicon of words and phrases to use in their own writing. We should challenge our brightest students; scaffold the lowest; and spend time reading, analyzing, and practicing sentences produced by skilled writers.

Until students practice crafting sentences, until they have worked with a variety of forms, phrases, and clauses and have learned to experiment with the various ways these elements can be creatively arranged and assembled, until they possess a lexicon of phrasing patterns in their minds to work with, one cannot expect students to produce reliably correct and sophisticated language patterns in their writing (Pudewa, 2004). These must be systematically and sequentially taught, and then practiced. With plenty of practice, one can learn to play a violin piece by heart. Practice is also the key to learning to write from memory—to see and hear in your mind what a proper sentence or paragraph looks and sounds like. In time, students will be able to create original thoughts and produce novel compositions that convey meaning in a creative and interesting way.

New research on how the brain works reveals that language and music lie side by side, sharing similar syntactical processes. Perhaps a study into the neuroscience of the language–music relationship could provide insight into a different approach to writing instruction (Li & Brand 2009; Patel, 2003).

4

Linguistic and Musical Syntax

Recent neuroimaging studies reveal that linguistic and musical syntax are similarly processed in the brain. Li and Brand (2009) report:

> Not only are language and musical processing located in the same area of the brain, but neurologists Maess and Koelsch (2001), have discovered that both musical and linguistic syntax are similarly processed. Music and language are of course dramatically different forms of communication. However, as Ayotte (2004) observed, "Both music and language share the same auditory perceptive and cognitive mechanism that impose structure on auditory information received by the senses." (p. 10)

Neuroscientist Aniruddh D. Patel (2003) found that language and music overlap in many ways. He hypothesizes, "Syntax in language and music share a common set of processes (instantiated in frontal brain areas) that operate on different structural representations (in posterior brain areas)" (p. 674). Music and language have syntax, because each has a set of principles that govern how discrete structural elements are combined into sequences. These sequences are not created haphazardly, but combine through orderly syntactical relationships. Patel (2003) elaborates:

> Combinatorial principles operate at multiple levels, such as the formation of words, phrases, and sentences in language, and of chords, chord progression, and keys in music. . . . Together with other types of information, syntactic knowledge allows the mind to accomplish a remarkable transformation of the input: a linear sequence of elements is perceived in terms of hierarchical relations that convey organized patterns of meaning. (p. 674)

Neuroscientists have found that although language and music have distinct and specific representations (phoneme/note, words/chords, sentences/musical phrases), they are both generative phrasing systems that share neural resources for activating and integrating these representations during syntactic processing (Brown, Martinez, & Parsons, 2006; Maess & Koelsch, 2001; Patel, 2003). Basically, neuroimaging data documents that language and music operate side-by-side in the brain.

AUDIATION THEORY FOR MUSIC AND WRITING

Because neuroscientists have discovered a syntactical relationship between language and music, innovative educators could look to experts on music skills acquisition in order to find parallels for writing skills acquisition. Because both sets of skills share parallel processing systems and resources, both could also share a similar pedagogy for skills acquisition. In 2003, Edwin Gordon presented a new theory in his book on music learning theory, which he called *audiation.* Audiation is to music what thought is to writing. It is the intellectual process that enables one to produce novel patterns of thought as we write words or compose music.

Students learn to audiate and to perform music as a result of sequential music instruction and years of practice. Eventually they develop a large enough lexicon of musical phrases and songs that they begin to truly understand music. This process is no different from the process we go through as we learn to think in words and to communicate those thoughts through writing. Gordon (2003) relates:

> Just as words are the smallest units of meaning in language, understood by young children long before they understand phrases, sentences, poems, or stories; tonal patterns and rhythm patterns are the smallest units of meaning in music and so must be assimilated first. Learning to listen to and to identify patterns in music is what prepares students to listen to and to perform standard music literature with understanding, rather than simply learning it by rote and imitating or memorizing it without giving it musical meaning. By giving meaning to music, students are not only able to perform great music of others, they can compose their own. Moreover, they are able to look at notation and know what it sounds like before they play it on an instrument or hear someone else perform it for them. (p. x)

Unlike reading, the process of writing requires being able to recall "by ear" complex language patterns. Visualize a vocalist preparing to perform a song. Before the singer can recall a piece from memory, it first has to be cemented in the mind through the ear. Through practice and focused listening, the song becomes committed to memory. Then it may be performed. Suzuki (2007), a well-known music teacher, understood the importance of learning by ear. He introduced the violin to very young children by using size-appropriate instruments. Students listened to tape recordings when practicing at home. Suzuki combined reading music with training by ear.

Writing requires a similar kind of training by ear. Music educator Allison Garner (2009) quotes Edwin Gordon's definition of *audiation*: "Audiation requires the ability to hear with discernment and 'play back' what is heard or created inside one's own head" (p. 1). When speaking or writing, how many times have we asked, "Does that sound right?" Gordon (2003) associated the activities of "writing from memory, performing from memory, and creating or improvising while writing" (p. 1) as associated with the audiation process.

Musician and writing instructor Andrew Pudewa (2004) stated in a lecture that students need to hear reliably correct and sophisticated language patterns as a foundation for writing them. He stressed the importance of reading a large variety of literature aloud. Before the age of television, reading aloud, often for hours, was a common way to pass the evening.

Oral-based indigenous societies, such as Native American tribes, have a similar practice called *storytelling*. The elders, as the culture bearers, could take days to complete a story. Through listening, youth acquired the beautifully complex language patterns unique to their cultural conventions. Audiation is the intellectual process that enables one to creatively reproduce the complex patterns previously learned by ear, whether through song, instrument, storytelling, or writing.

In the article "The Movement of Air, the Breath of Meaning: Aurality and Multimodal Composing," Cynthia Selfe (2009) explores the history of aural composition modalities of speech, music, and sound. She argues for a "relationship between aurality, the visual modalities, and writing . . . and its importance to different communities and cultures" (p. 616). Explaining a change that has occurred in college English departments during the last half of the nineteenth century, Selfe (2009) perceived the following shift away from aurality (listening) and talking (orality):

> The power of vision and print gradually waxed in context of a university education, the power of aurality gradually waned. . . . Writing and reading, for example, became separated from speech in educational contexts and became largely silent practices for students in classroom settings. Written literature . . . was studied through silent reading and subjected to written analysis, consumed by the eye rather than the ear. (pp. 622–623)

Our experiences with college English classes have, indeed, focused on reading, on critical analysis, and reader response, typically exercises in quietness.

The writer's workshop should offer a wide range of opportunities for students to hear and to orally practice the complex language patterns they will need in their writing, yet our academic experience has been predominantly a silent one—we write, we trade papers, we edit, and we rewrite.

Richard Fulkerson (2001), an author and the Director of English Graduate Programs at Texas A&M, wrote:

> What the various post-process and "social" pedagogies have in common is that they don't "teach writing" (in the sense of explaining various invention and revision tactics for students and directing the student to practice using them) but do require it, while focusing on reading instead. (p. 113)

Writing is more than just sophisticated reading. Writing skills acquisition begins with hearing reliably correct and sophisticated language patterns (Pudewa, 2004), and then practicing them, to orally produce complex forms, phrases, and clauses, and to write them. Through reading aloud and oral-based guided practice, one eventually learns to audiate thoughts from a rich reservoir of words that one hears in one's mind.

Although Gordon's (2003) audiation theory is a music learning theory, it could just as easily describe a writing learning theory. Although Gordon's first aim was to explain the process of music skills acquisition, one could also use audiation theory to help explain the process of writing skills acquisition. Gordon's second goal was to help parents understand music learning theory. The goal of this book is to offer educators a new way of looking at our pedagogy for writing.

The process for audiating language and music is the same (Gordon, 2003). Both take time and require years of practice and study. The process is systematic and sequential. Students begin by listening to and practicing the simplest elements and then moving to more complex forms. One learns to audiate from the outside in. We cannot perform from memory a composition that we have not practiced and learned, just as we cannot spontaneously produce well-structured phrases if we have not practiced and learned a variety of phrases. Although we may read an interesting and complex phrase, if we do not practice using it in our writing or speaking, it is quickly forgotten.

Memorization is not audiation, either. Gordon (2003) asserts, "Audiation is an excitingly circular, back and forth motion, and not at all like imitation and memorization, which are boringly linear" (p. 6). To imitate what someone else wrote is simply dictation, but one must write and practice what others write before one has the ability to produce novel work. Gordon (2003) declares, "When a person learns how to audiate, imitation and memorization become unnecessary" (p. 6).

David Brooks (2011), a journalist for the *New York Times*, has always been fascinated with research about the mind and how the brain works. In his book *The Social Animal*, he relates research comparing novice chess players to grandmasters. In one experiment, both novices and experts were shown a series of chessboards for about five to ten seconds apiece. On each board about twenty pieces were arranged as if it were an actual game. The participants were later asked to remember where each piece was on the board. The grandmasters remembered every piece, whereas the novices remembered only four or five pieces per board. However, when the pieces were placed randomly on the board, in a way that did not relate to any game situation, the grandmasters could not remember any better than the novices. Brooks (2011) explained:

> The real reason the grandmasters could remember the game boards so well is that after so many years of study, they saw the boards in a different way. When average players saw the boards, they saw a group of individual pieces. When the masters saw the boards, they saw formations. Instead of seeing a bunch of letters on a page, they saw words, paragraphs, and stories. A story is easier to remember than a bunch of letters. Expertise is about forming internal connections so that little pieces of information turn into bigger networked chunks of information. Learning is not merely about accumulating facts. It is internalizing the relationships between pieces of information. . . . Every field has its own structure, its own schema of big ideas, organizing principles, and recurring patterns—in short, its own paradigm. The expert has absorbed this structure and has a tacit knowledge of how to operate within it. . . . At first the expert decided to enter a field of study, but soon the field entered her. (pp. 88–89)

What a beautiful analogy for the process of audiation! One sets out to master a discipline by devoting years of study and practice to individual elements or series of elements. In the beginning, learning a discipline is hard work. Eventually one begins to see, feel, and experience the relationship between elements, and one can see in one's mind how they all relate and fit together. Then, suddenly, the element or discipline seems easy.

For instance, after one masters a back handspring, it seems simple. But to learn a back handspring takes a lot of focus and hard work. A novice has to think about the series of movements in her mind, one-by-one, before she attempts it. A spotter scaffolds her attempts many times before a gymnast gains the confidence to try it solo. For the beginner, one back handspring feels scary, complicated, and difficult, but for the expert, it is as easy as skipping. As Brooks (2011) insightfully concludes, "The result is that the expert doesn't think more about a subject, she thinks less. Because she has domain expertise, she anticipates how things will fit together" (p. 89).

To summarize audiation theory, we have taken the liberty to paraphrase a paradigm for written audiation from Gordon's (2003) work on music audiation:

> The ability to spontaneously compose creative and well-structured works of writing is called *written audiation*. If you are able to hear the organization of complex language patterns of thought and give syntactical meaning to your thoughts before you write them, then you are engaging in written audiation. Written audiation could be further defined as the cognitive processing of complex language patterns from physical memory with the ability to organize and compose original thought using innovative structure and syntax. Authors, who can audiate, are able to bring meaning to their thoughts through written expression by using a variety of phrases that follow a natural flow of rhythm, structure, and style. Audiation is an understanding of the flow of words. Some may even discern that great writing is like the music of words.

How do we teach sentence-level writing?

I.   Dress-Ups
1. Quality adjective
2. Who/which clause
3. Strong verb
4. "ly" word
5. Prepositional phrase
6. Adverb clause

II. Sentence Openers
1. Subject
2. Prepositional phrase
3. "ly" word
4. "ing" word
5. Adverb clause
6. VSS (very short sentence, two to five words)
7. "ed" word

III. Decorations
1. Question
2. Conversation
3. 3sss (three short staccato sentences)
4. Dramatic opening and closing
5. Simile and metaphor
6. Alliteration

5

Ingham-Webster-Pudewa Method

As we mentioned in chapter 2, we were introduced to sentence-level writing through Pudewa's seminar *Teaching Writing: Structure and Style* (2015). Through extensive modeling and guided practice, we were taught how to use and teach this systematic method for writing. Although a strictly written presentation is less than optimal, we will endeavor to describe the foundational elements that circumscribe sentence-level writing. As with any method, it is much easier to grasp when one can see it modeled and receive guided practice. We will, however, try our best to present a verbal picture of this primer for writing skills acquisition. We hope to demonstrate for educators and writers of all ages how writing instruction can, indeed, be explicit and comprehensible.

DRESS-UPS

Teaching the art of crafting interesting sentences begins with introducing the forms, phrases, and clauses that make up sentences. Webster (1994) calls the elements found within a sentence *Dress-Ups* because we are asking students to "dress up" their writing in very specific ways. Dress-Ups are introduced and practiced one at a time. Webster's (1994) Dress-Ups include the following elements:

1. Quality adjective
2. Who/which clause
3. Strong verb
4. "ly" word

5. Prepositional phrase
6. Adverb clause (when, while, where, as, since, if, although, because). (p. 39)

Levels of Instruction

Levels for this writing method are not age or grade dependent, but are skills dependent. They are progressive, building one on the other. Once students have mastered the elements required for a level, they move to the next. Because elementary teachers have a new batch of students every year, students must start each school year at level one of the method. Even those who teach consecutive grades will probably have new students every year, and if so, she or he will need to start everyone at the first level. Obviously, older students will be able to progress much more quickly through the levels than younger ones.

Level 1: Quality Adjectives, Because Clause, Who/Which Clause

Sentence-level instruction should begin in kindergarten. Once students can write a basic sentence, the teacher may begin introducing Dress-Ups. Using one of her "read alouds" of the day as a springboard, the teacher may choose a key noun from the story to introduce *quality adjectives*. Drawing a word web on the board, the teacher may ask the students to brainstorm quality adjectives to describe the key noun as the teacher writes them on the word web.

If the "read aloud" is "The Three Little Pigs," the teacher might put the word *wolf* on the board and ask the students to brainstorm words to describe the wolf. Next the teacher may create a sentence frame leaving the quality adjective blank; the students must pick one of the adjectives that were brainstormed and finish the sentence. The sentence frame might look like this:

The _____ wolf wanted to _____.

The *because clause* is another element that can be taught and practiced in kindergarten. Again the teacher could create the following sentence frames:

I like _____ **because** _____.
The _____ wolf wanted to _____ **because** _____.

Once students are consistently incorporating quality adjectives and the because clause, the teacher can introduce the *who/which clause*. Using the posted classroom alphabet letter or picture cards, students can be asked to finish the following type of sentence frame for each letter of the alphabet:

A is for apple, **which** _____.
B is for bear, **who** _____.
C is for cat, **who** _____.

A more advanced version of this activity is to have the students brainstorm quality adjectives for the alphabet word, and include a who/which clause. The sentence frames are structured as follows:

D is for a/the _____ dog, **who** _____.
E is for a/the _____ egg, **which** _____.
F is for a/the _____ fish, **who** _____.

Level II: Strong Verb, "ly" Word, Prepositional Phrase, Adverb Clause; Key Word Outline, Oral Retelling, Writing Matrix, Paragraph Clinchers, Composition Check Sheet

Once students start first grade, the first two Dress-Ups should be taught and reviewed and then Dress-Ups three through six should be introduced, one at a time, and then practiced. Beginning in first grade, students may be taught how to summarize a piece of text by creating a Key Word Outline. Instead of the teacher choosing the key noun from the "read aloud," students are taught how to find the contentives (key words) from informational text through key word outlining.

Key Word Outline. Using the most pertinent information from the "read aloud," the teacher takes the information that she or he really wants the students to know and remember and prepares a simple summary paragraph of four to six sentences in length on chart paper or on the board. After the teacher presents the "read aloud" to the class, she asks the students to perform a "shared read aloud" of the paragraph summary. Next, beginning with the first sentence, the teacher will model how to choose three key words from the sentence that will help one to best remember the main idea. The teacher underlines the contentives with a marker.

The teacher also demonstrates how to record the contentives in Key Word Outline format. She creates the Key Word Outline on the board or on chart paper, while the students record their Key Word Outline on a 3-by-5-inch notecard. For the remaining sentences, the teacher will call on students to model this exercise. As individual students are called on to read a sentence and to choose the key words, the rest of the students write either the underlined selections or their own selections of key words on their notecard.

Numbers and symbols are free, which means students do not have to count them as key words. Dates, numbers, symbols, and signs do not count, and pictorial figures can be used sparingly. For instance, if the sentence is long, a stick figure may be used to represent *person, people, world, man, men, woman,*

Textbox 5.1. Key Word Outline Format

Title

By: _____

I. _____, _____, _____ (topic sentence)
   1. _____, _____, _____ (detail)
   2. _____, _____, _____ (detail)
   3. _____, _____, _____ (detail)
   4. _____, _____, _____ (detail)
   5. _____, _____, _____ (clincher sentence)

---

women, or *group*. Or a circle with a slash symbol through it could stand for *no, none, nothing,* or *not*. The Key Word Outline format can be seen in textbox 5.1.

If the teacher chose to read aloud Jim Arnosky's (2008) *All About Turtles,* a sample Paragraph Summary (the bold words are the key words the students selected and underlined) and sample Key Word Outline may be seen in textboxes 5.2 and 5.3, respectively.

After the students have found the key words for every sentence, students take turns *retelling* the text from their Key Word Outlines. The teacher covers the original paragraph or erases it, and then the students are asked to

---

Textbox 5.2. Sample Paragraph Summary

All About Turtles
By: Mrs. Hatfield

Turtles are **reptiles with shells.** Like all reptiles, they are **cold-blooded** so they cannot **regulate** their body **temperature** from within. **Worldwide,** there are more than **200 types** of turtles. They can be grouped into three types: **saltwater** turtles; **freshwater** turtles; and **land-dwelling** turtles, called *tortoises*. The turtle's top **shell** is called a **carapace** and the bottom is called the **plastron.** On **females** the plastron is convex like a **smile;** on males it is concave like a **frown.** A turtle's **skin** is **sensitive** like **ours.** Turtles can live **long lives,** sometimes up to **100 years.** Turtles have **survived** on our **planet** since the dawn of **dinosaurs.**

> **Textbox 5.3. Sample Key Word Outline**
>
> Turtles
> By:_____
>
> I.   reptiles, with, shells
> 1. cold-blooded, regulate, temperature
> 2. worldwide, <200, types
> 3. saltwater, freshwater, land-dwelling
> 4. shell, carapace, plastron
> 5. female, smile, frown
> 6. skin, sensitive, ours
> 7. long, lives, 100 years
> 8. survived, planet, dinosaurs

reformulate each sentence from its contentives. This *oral retelling* provides presentation practice and it forces students to summarize the text using their own words before actually having to write a summary.

Writing Matrix. Before asking students to write, the teacher should ask the class to brainstorm possible forms, phrases, and clauses to use in their writing. Students are asked to choose two or three key nouns and verbs from their Key Word Outline and to insert them into the *Writing Matrix,* which is posted on the board. The students brainstorm only those Dress-Ups that have been introduced. Assuming that all of the Dress-Ups have been taught, a sample Writing Matrix for the "turtle" write might look something like table 5.1.

We have included a full-sized blank template of the Writing Matrix in Appendix B.

After the students have selected their first key noun, such as "turtle," they are asked to brainstorm a few quality adjectives to describe turtles and record them in the Writing Matrix. When they have exhausted their ideas, they are asked to brainstorm some possible who/which clauses to further describe their topic. Next students are asked to consider whether the verb they selected is a strong verb. If the verb was a boring one like "sat," the teacher would ask the students to think of more descriptive verbs, such as "crouched," "perched," "squatted," or "sprawled."

Once they have chosen a strong verb, such as "survived," the teacher asks the students to brainstorm a few *"ly" words* or adverbs to describe how, in what way, and to what degree the turtles survived. Then students brainstorm *prepositional phrases* by asking questions like where, when, and in what direction

Table 5.1. Sample Writing Matrix

Quality Adjective	Noun	"ly" Word	Strong Verb
cold-blooded interesting saltwater freshwater land-dwelling reserved reclusive shy	turtles	tenaciously remarkably surprisingly miraculously	survived
hard bony plated tough curved domed tough	shells		
sensitive human-like	skin		

Who/Which Clause

plastron, **which** on females curves up like a smile and on males curves down like a frown
land-dwellers, **which** are called tortoises

Prepositional Phrase

reptiles **with** shells
survived **on** our planet/**through** the centuries
more than 200 types of turtles

www.asia.b (when, while, where, as, since, if, although, because)

since the dawn of dinosaurs
plastron . . . **while** on males it curves down like a frown
You can tell males from females **because** their plastrons are different.
While their shells are tough, their skin is extremely sensitive.

(time wise) the turtles survived. In the "turtle" summary, the verb "survived" is followed by the prepositional phrase "on the planet," so students may use that one or choose one of the other prepositions in the Writing Matrix.

Students could also brainstorm some possible *adverb clauses*. Again, they may use the one included in the summary, "since the dawn of dinosaurs," but they should also brainstorm a few original selections in order to have choices. The students do not have to brainstorm every element in the Writing Matrix for each key noun/verb selected. For instance, if the students brainstormed several prepositional phrases for the "turtles/survived" kernel, the teacher may choose to skip brainstorming prepositional phrases for the next noun/verb selected, and instead focus on adverb clauses. The purpose of this exercise is to provide examples and choices for each element that the teacher is expecting students to incorporate in their writing.

Once all of the sentence elements have been brainstormed in the Writing Matrix, students are ready to write. In the beginning of the school year, the teacher should lead the exercise by having the class perform a shared write. The teacher first models how to reconstruct the text from the Key Word Outline and Writing Matrix and demonstrates how to incorporate Dress-Ups as she or he writes. Next, the teacher asks students to volunteer to model for the class. To indicate that a Dress-Up has been used, the teacher demonstrates that Dress-Ups are underlined. The rule is that only one of each kind of Dress-Up is underlined per paragraph. So although the students may use more than one quality adjective, they only underline one.

Paragraph Clinchers. As the teacher and students reach the end of their shared write, the teacher introduces *paragraph clinchers*. A paragraph clincher restates the main idea from the topic sentence. For the "turtle" write, students might create the following paragraph clinchers:

> "Turtles are the only reptiles born with their house on their back."
> "Maybe turtles have survived so long because they are born with armor on their back."
> "How interesting that turtles come topped with a stout, shelly shelter!"

When students are finished with their shared write, the teacher may introduce the Composition Checksheet. This is an assessment rubric for students and teachers to use. The teacher models how to self-check by progressing systematically through the lists on the Checksheet. Students put a check mark next to each required element to ensure that their paragraph is complete before moving on to peer editing. A Composition Checksheet for classroom use may be found in Appendix C.

As soon as students attain an understanding of the method, the teacher will have them write with a partner. For those who still need support, the teacher may continue to scaffold learning by facilitating a shared write. Once students are ready, they should be encouraged to write independently. After the brainstorming session for the Writing Matrix, the goal is to move all students into the independent phase.

A fun activity to practice brainstorming Dress-Ups is to put a simple kernel sentence on the board like, "The frog sat." The teacher puts the "frog/sat" in the Writing Matrix in the "noun/verb" columns. Then she may ask the students to brainstorm the following elements, while the teacher records their responses into the Writing Matrix:

1. Quality adjectives to describe the frog
2. Who/which clauses to further describe the frog

3. Strong verbs for "sat"
4. "ly" words for how and in what way the frog sat
5. Prepositional phrases for where, when, and what direction the frog sat
6. Adverb clauses (when, while, where, as, if, since, although, because) to further describe how the frog sat

Have the students use Dress-Ups one through six to create one complex sentence. A few examples of dressed-up sentences follow:

"The famished frog carefully crouched on a lily pad in the evening while patiently waiting for a fly."
"The frisky frog playfully perched on a lily pad when her best friend arrived."
"The frightened frog silently squatted on a lily pad because a water snake was slithering by."
"The fat, freckled frog sprawled lazily on her lily pad, although she should seek a safer spot for a nap."

Not only are the Dress-Up expectations posted for all to see, but also examples for each are brainstormed by the whole class, so in order for students to be successful, they only have to pick one from the board and insert it in their writing. This exercise helps to eliminate the "deer in the headlights" phenomenon when students actually sit down to write. There is nothing more terrifying than staring at a blank page, feeling as if you have a blank brain, while the expectation is that you must produce something intelligible.

Sentence Openers and Decorations

Level III: Sentence Openers

In second grade, after the students are consistently incorporating Dress-Ups, the teacher may begin to introduce the variety of ways one can open a sentence. Using the Writing Matrix, the teacher should demonstrate how various elements may be manipulated and rearranged to create a variety of Sentence Openers. Webster (1994) defines ten types of Sentence Openers in the following outline:

1. Subject
2. Prepositional phrase (preposition + noun)
3. "ly" word (adverb)
4. "ing" word (participial phrase)
5. Adverb clause (when, while, where, as, since, if, although, because)
6. Very short sentence (VSS) of two to five words
7. "ed" word (past participial phrase) (p. 39)

(?) Question (opens with a question)
(I!) Interjections (oh, ouch, wow, ha, ugh, aha)
(T,) Transitional (first, next, also, now, later, thus, then, indeed, however, therefore, otherwise, moreover, hence, furthermore, likewise, henceforth)

The following list demonstrates ten ways one may open a sentence, yet still communicate the same basic thought:

1. Subject: The frog sat on a lily pad.
2. Prepositional: In the evening the frog sat on a lily pad.
3. "ly" word: Anxiously, the frog sat on a lily pad.
4. "ing" word: Waiting patiently, the frog sat on a lily pad.
5. Adverb clause: While patiently waiting for a fly, the frog sat on a lily pad.
6. VSS: The frog sat.
7. "ed" word: Famished, the frog sat on a lily pad.

(?) Question: Did you see the fat frog on the lily pad?
(I!): Interjection: Alas! What a lazy fat frog!
(T,): Transitional: Hence, the frog just sat.

Phrase and clause manipulation is like playing a game with the order of elements. Using a variety of phrases and clauses affords myriad ways to create interesting Sentence Openers. See figure 5.1: Phrase and Clause Manipulation.

Again, Sentence Openers are introduced one at a time. In the first grade, the teacher may be able to introduce the first three Sentence Openers to

SENTENCE OPENERS		DRESS-UPS
(2) In the evening		famished
(3) Stealthily,		who was starving
(4) Crouching stealthily,	(1) The frog sat.	crouched
(5) While waiting for a fly,		stealthily crouched
(6) The frog sat.		on a lily pad in the evening
(7) Famished,		while waiting for a fly

Figure 5.1. **Phrase and Clause Manipulation**

some of her students, but most require the entire school year to master the Dress-Ups. In the case of a few accelerated learners or a few delayed learners, the teacher may differentiate the lessons through small-group instruction, while others are working with partners or independently. Students indicate which Sentence Opener they used by writing its corresponding number in the margin next to the opener and then circling it. This indicator makes it easy for students to self-check and for the teacher to quickly track each student's progress.

By the second grade, the teacher can encourage students to generate their own summary propositions from the "read aloud" by asking them either to sketch key ideas or to take notes on key points as the teacher reads. After the "read aloud," the teacher may ask students to create propositions from their sketches or notes, and basically write their own summary sentences. Once they have crafted their summary propositions, they may then identify their key words and generate a Key Word Outline. Then the method continues as before: orally retell, brainstorm Dress-Ups into the Writing Matrix, and write the rough draft with a partner or independently.

Decorations. These are special elements one may use to decorate one's writing. At any time the teacher feels it is appropriate, she or he may introduce a Decoration and require the students to use one. For instance, one could ask students to either open or close their paragraph with a question. Or the teacher may introduce similes and metaphors, or teach how to include conversation. Pudewa's (2015) Decorations are listed in the following outline:

1. Question
2. Conversation
3. 3sss
4. Dramatic opening and closing
5. Simile or metaphor
6. Alliteration (p. 171)

The 3sss are three short, staccato sentences with various word patterns. If the number in front of the sentence is 4:3:2, it means the first sentence has four words, the third three, and the last sentence two. Pudewa (2015) shares a few examples of 3sss.

> 4:3:2 Killer bees invaded America. Viciously they attacked. Humans suffered.
> 3:3:3 Savage bees attacked. Violently they killed. Nobody was spared.
> 2:2:2 Bees invaded. They marauded. Humans perished. (p. 184)

Dramatic opening and closing is a short, dramatic opening sentence, a VSS, before the topic sentence combined with another dramatic VSS after the clincher, such as the one we used in the analogy of the novice piano student, "The novice smiles. . . . The novice cries."

Similes compare two unlike things using the words "like" or "as." For example,

> "Her smile is as bright as a shiny new locket."
> "Our house is as quiet as an empty pants pocket."
> "Her hopes soared through the skies like a flaming red rocket."

Metaphors state one thing is something else and they do not contain the words "like" or "as." For example,

> "His heart is of stone, his words sharp and cutting."
> "She is swimming in a sea of troubles."
> "You are my sunshine, the apple of my eye!"

Alliteration uses three or more words with the same letter or letter blend sound. Alliteratives may be separated by conjunctions, articles, pronouns, or prepositions. For example,

> "What a bouncing bundle of baby boys!"
> "The tenacious tiny turtle trundled toward the sea. It clumsily clawed and clambered toward the crashing waves."
> "The ferocious fox fought fiercely for his family."

Another type of alliteration can be found in the last paragraph in chapter 19: "to aggregate . . . [,] to accommodate . . . [,] to advocate" (Hatfield & Young, 2015, p. 123). Decorations should be used sparingly, "as an artist might add a splash of bright color to a nature painting" (Pudewa, 2015, p. 184). As their name implies, Decorations are used to accent and enliven prose, but should be limited to one per paragraph.

Level IV: Report and Essay Writing, Introductory Paragraph, Concluding Paragraph, Titles, Final Clinchers

During the third through fifth grade years, the goal for the sentence-level intervention is to introduce and practice all of the Dress-Ups, Sentence Openers, and Decorations, and to start writing multiple paragraph essays and reports.

Report and Essay Writing. Students are taught how to look for three sources and find three themes. Sources could be books, articles, or an online encyclopedia reference. Once students have found three themes, they make a Key Word Outline for each one from each source. Next they are taught how to fuse their nine theme outlines into one outline for each theme, and then to write from the three fused outlines. For instance, if the student wanted to do a research report on turtles, his three themes could be saltwater turtles, freshwater turtles, and land dwellers.

Students would select sources that contain information about all three types of turtles. From each source students create a Key Word Outline for each type of turtle, ending up with a total of nine Key Word Outlines. Once that was done, they fuse the three outlines for each type of turtle. For example, for the three outlines (one from each source) for saltwater turtles, students would choose six to eight key points that they feel are most important from the three outlines and fuse them into one outline. They will do the same for the three outlines for the freshwater and land-dwelling turtles, so that students end up with three Key Word Outlines, which contain the information that they most want to write about.

Now the method continues as before. Students brainstorm a Writing Matrix Worksheet for each Key Word Outline. For this activity, the students may ask for help from a partner if they feel they need it. Those students who are slower verbal processors should partner with students who have an aptitude for brainstorming words so that peers may help scaffold one another. From the three Key Word Outlines and the three Writing Matrix Worksheets, the student writes the rough draft. Using the Composition Checksheet, students self-check to see if they have included all the required elements. Next they edit with a partner, then edit with the teacher, and then write the final draft.

For the five-paragraph essay and the research report, students are taught how to create an introductory and concluding paragraph. The *introductory paragraph* gives background, including time and place, and states the three themes. The *concluding paragraph* repeats the three themes, telling which is the most important and why, and includes the *final clincher*.

Final Clincher. When compositions have multiple paragraphs, the concluding paragraph requires a *final clincher* sentence. A final clincher should restate the key words of the title and the topic sentence. A jingle to help students remember this rule is "For a *final clincher*, three things must equate: the title, the topic, and the clincher MUST RELATE!" Dr. Webster (1994) created an array of formulae and chants that graphically teach the rules of written communication (see Appendix E).

Titles. A great title recaps or summarizes the main idea of the topic sentence in a clever, creative, and succinct way. Creating effective final clinchers and titles is like playing a game with words. With a little practice, children become quite adept at creating especially clever expressions for these elements. For the "turtle" write, possible title ideas include,

"Tenacious Turtles"
"Three Types of Turtles"
"Turtles, Terrapins, and Tortoises"

The Institute for Excellence in Writing offers in-depth instruction for a variety of structural models in their seminars. Students receive training and practice writing book reports and critiques, writing from pictures, and writing five-paragraph essays, as well as tackling the super essay, which combines two or three complete five-paragraph essays into one paper. For instance, the "turtle" write could be expanded into a super essay by writing a five-paragraph essay for each type of turtle. The student would select three subthemes for each turtle, such as habitat, predators, and life cycle. The following models, taught in Pudewa's (2015) *Teaching Writing: Structure and Style,* outline the Basic Report/Essay Model, Critique Model (table 5.2), and Super Essay Model (table 5.3):

The Basic Report/Essay Model

Title
I. **Introduction**
   Grab Attention!
   Introduce subject and give background information, time, and place
   Thesis statement—state three topics—an essay map
II. **Topic Sentence A**
   1.
   2. details, examples, facts,
   3. explanations of topic
   4.
   5.
   Clincher (repeats or reflects two or three key words of Topic Sentence)
III. **Topic Sentence B**
   1.
   2. details, examples, facts
   3. explanations of topic
   4.
   5.

Clincher (repeats or reflects two or three key words of Topic Sentence)
IV. **Topic Sentence C**
   1.
   2. details, examples, facts
   3. explanations of topic
   4.
   5.
   Clincher (repeats or reflects two or three key words of Topic Sentence)
V. **Conclusion**
   Restate three topics
   Tell which is most significant and why
   Final Clincher (reflects opening topic and title)
   (Adapted from Pudewa, 2015, p. 130.)

Outlines make an otherwise daunting task more palatable for students. If they can see organized structure for the assignment, then they can visualize a way to the end of it. Outlines help capture the abstract idea of the whole and capsulate the process into concrete steps. They help demystify the process of writing for students. Providing writing models scaffold student success.

SCAFFOLDING COMMON CORE STATE STANDARDS FOR WRITING

Common Core State Standards for Writing K–5 asks students to write in a variety of genres. Students are required to use descriptive details, linking words and phrases, effective techniques, organized structure, and concluding statements, with each element supporting the writer's purpose. To do this, students need direct, explicit instruction and lots of guided practice working with these individual elements and structures, and they need to see outlines, rubrics, and models that define and describe what is required of them. With ample support and practice, children develop a lexicon of writing elements

Table 5.2. Critique Model

Introduction: (Grab attention, give basic information about the book: author, title, genre)
I. Characters, Setting: (Describe: time, place, characters, purpose, mood)
II. Conflict, Plot: (State: problem, surprise, plans, actions toward solution)
III. Climax, Theme: (Describe: turning point, how is problem solved, message)
Conclusion: (Like/dislike? Why/why not? Theme/moral? Never use "I")

Table 5.3. Super Essay Model

		Bountiful Bananas
Title		
By: Name		By: Webster
Super-Introduction	Gives background (BG), Time (T), Place (P); States 3 Themes (3Th)	A. History B. Eating C. Growing and Handling
Intro Essay A (1, 2, 3)	BG/T/P; States 3 subthemes (3sTh)	History: A1. Migration A2. Varieties A3. Gros Michael
Topic A1	Topic sentence (TS) Details (DT) Clincher sentence (CS)	A1. Migration
Topic A2	TS/DT/CS	A2. Varieties
Topic A3	TS/DT/CS	A3. Gros Michael
Conclusion Essay A	Restate 3sTh. Tell which is most important and why (MI/Y), final CS	Gros Michael favorite, travels well, large, prolific
Intro Essay B (1, 2, 3)	BG/T/P; State 3sTh	Eating: B1. Plantain B2. Gros Michael B3. Nutrition
Topic B1	TS/DT/CS	B1. Plantain
Topic B2	TS/DT/CS	B2. Gros Michael
Topic B3	TS/DT/CS	B3. Nutrition
Conclusion Essay B	Restate 3sTh/MI/Y/Final CS	Most bananas vegetable; Gros Michael fruit, nutritious, digestible
Intro Essay C (1, 2, 3)	BG/T/P; State 3sTh	Growing/Handling: C1. Plantations C2. Shipping C3. Home Care
Topic C1	TS/DT/CS	C1. Plantations
Topic C2	TS/DT/CS	C2. Shipping
Topic C3	TS/DT/CS	C3. Home Care
Conclusion Essay C	Restate 3sTh/MI/Y/Final CS	Grown in tropics, shipped by boat, must be treated carefully
Super-Conclusion	Restate 3Th/MI/Y/Final CS	History 2,000 yr., eaten/shipped—world, versatile use, tasty, bountiful

(Webster, 1994, p. 217)

and structures that prepare them to master the requirements of Common Core State Standards.

By strengthening writing skills acquisition at the sentence level, we lay a foundation that scaffolds desired writing outcomes at the paragraph level and beyond. This writing intervention provides students a primer for how to begin, a blueprint for where they are going, and a scaffold for what success looks like. It provides students stylistic techniques, structural models, and precisely defined rubrics that explain the craft of writing. The precursor for mastering the new writing standards begins with learning to write at the sentence level.

6

Writers

Middle School, High School, College, and Beyond

Although this intervention is primarily geared toward elementary students, sentence-level writing instruction is just as valuable for middle school, high school, and college students, as well as for parents, business people, administrators, or anyone who has to put words down on paper. If your job, profession, or position requires you to pen something in written form, then this intervention will help you to produce more accomplished and sophisticated compositions.

Those who are able to express themselves well are generally perceived as more intelligent and are more likely to advance. The pen has the power to persuade, to move people to action, and to get us the things we want and need. The art of skillfully crafting sentences and paragraphs may benefit anyone who needs to write.

Leta has created an extended version of Webster's (1994) techniques for secondary and postsecondary writing instruction that will assist most writers. For example, in the following outline (see p. 43) of advanced stylistic techniques for seasoned writers, she introduces cumulative syntax. A cumulative sentence is an independent clause followed by subordinate clauses or phrases that provide more details, descriptions, or information about the main person, place, idea, or event.

If one has a lot to say, but can use only a sentence or two, one may do it if one understands the cumulative sentence. To use a cumulative sentence, begin with a base clause and follow it with a series of modifying phrases that may begin with "a," "an," "the," an "ing" word, an "ed" word, an "ly" word, "to" with a verb, or possessive pronouns "he," "she," "his," "her," or "its." In *Heart of Darkness*, Joseph Conrad (1990) uses cumulative sentences in the following passage:

> Marlow sat cross-legged right aft, leaning against the mizzenmast. He had sunken cheeks, a yellow complexion, a straight back, an ascetic aspect, and, with arms dropped, the palms of hands outwards, resembled an idol. (Conrad, 1990, p. 1)

As in this example, seasoned writers may experiment and expand their style by occasionally including cumulative syntax. To practice writing cumulative sentences, Professor Brooks Landon (2008) in his book *Building Better Sentences* created the following sentence frames:

1. Big Al headed back into the bar,
    a. a_____,
    b. his_____,
    c. _____(ing)_____,
    d. to_____(<- verb)_____,
    e. he_____.
2. They sat down at the table,
    a. he_____,
    b. his_____,
    c. his_____,
    d. she_____,
    e. her_____,
    f. her_____,
    g. the table_____,
    h. its_____,
    i. its_____,
    j. the overall scene suggesting_____.
   (p. 49)

Landon (2008) introduced writers to the cumulative, the suspensive, and the balanced sentence. The suspensive sentence is a cumulative that suspends the base clause until the very end. He gives an example of a sentence that uses cumulative syntax to create suspense.

> He drove the car carefully, his shaggy hair whipped by the wind, his eyes hidden behind wraparound shades, his mouth set in a grim smile, a .38 Police Special on the seat beside him, the corpse stuffed in the trunk.

The balanced sentence provides a challenge for students as well. Landon (2008) instructs, "A balanced sentence hinges in the middle, usually split by a semicolon, the second half of the sentence paralleling the first half, but changing one or two key words or altering word order" (p. 83). Consider these familiar examples.

When the going gets tough, the tough get going.
Short words are best and old short words when short are best of all.
—Winston Churchill
Ask not what your country can do for you; ask what you can do for your country. —John F. Kennedy

For seasoned writers, Leta provides the following list of advanced stylistic techniques, which will challenge and benefit writers of all ages:

ADVANCED STYLISTIC TECHNIQUES

I. **Dress-Ups**
   1. **Quality adjectives:**
      Tramping over the **misty damp** heath was exhilarating!
   2. **Who/which clause:** (adjective clause)
      My husband, **who** loves fly fishing, is a serious angler.
   3. **Strong verb:** (image or feeling!)
      The tiger voraciously **devoured** its kill.
   4. **"ly" word:** (adverb word)
      The **frightfully** frumpy old woman slumped **dispiritedly** on the park bench.
   5. **Adverb clause:** (subordinating conjunctions) [When, where, while, as, since, if, although, because, after, as if, as much as, as long as, as soon as, before, in order that, lest, so that, than that, though, unless, until, whenever, wherever, whether]
      The gopher tortoise is shy, **although** sometimes he shares his burrow with a rattlesnake.
   6. **Noun clause:** [that, what, whoever, whatever, of what]
      She never imagined **that** she would be a princess.
   7. **Dual verbs, "ly" words, or adjectives:**
      He **lazily** and **leisurely** napped in the **warm summer** sunshine.
   8. **Appositive:** (renames the noun)
      My mother, **a registered nurse,** actually had a weak stomach for trauma and gore.

II. *Sentence Openers*
   1. **Subject: Leta** and **Eulalie** absolutely adore horses.
   2. **Prepositional phrase:** [aboard, about, above, according to, across, after, against, along, amid, among, around, aside, at, because of, before, behind, below, beneath, beside, between, beyond, by, concerning, despite, down, during, except, for, from, in, inside, instead, into, like, minus, near, of, off, on opposite, out, outside,

over, past, since, through, throughout, to, toward, under, underneath, unlike, until, up, upon, with, within, without]
On a gorgeous wintery day, we walked over the river and through the woods to Gram's house for Christmas dinner.
3. **"ly" word:** (adverbs) **Eventually** the children learned to write.
4. **"-ing" word:** (present participial phrase followed by the subject)
Running for her life, the mouse ducked under a log.
5. **"ed," "d, "en," "t," or "n" words:** (past participial phrase followed by the subject) [example: recovered, confused, eaten, dealt, driven]
Exhausted, the mouse took a moment to rest.
6. **Adverb Clause:** (adverbial subordinating conjunctions) [when, where, while, as, since, if, although, because, after, as if, as much as, as long as, as soon as, before, in order that, lest, so that, than that, though, unless, until, whenever, wherever, whether]
While the mouse rested, the cat lost interest and left.
1. **Very short sentence (VSS):** (two to five words with a strong verb)
The mouse rested.
2. **To + verb:** (infinitive phrase)
To escape the cat's clutches, the mouse had to use her wits.
3. **That, What, If:** (noun clauses introduced by signal words) [... why, how, where, whether, who, whom, whose, which, when, whoever, whomever, whichever, whatever]
Whether that really happened, is anyone's guess.
4. **It, There:** (Explicative, slot filler)
It looms ominously. **There** is no escape.
5. **If/then, Either/or, Whether/or:** (coordinating conjunctions) [Neither/nor, Both/and, Not only/but also, Just as/so too]
Either give me your answer, **or** I will do what I think is best.
(?) **Question: Did** you know Baskir Curly horses are hypoallergenic?
(!) **Interjection: Wow!** Isn't that interesting?
(T,) **Transitional: Furthermore,** their hair structure lacks a protein found in normal horse hair.

III. **Decorations** (one per paragraph)
1. **Question:** Did you know that Abraham Lincoln only had one year of formal schooling?
2. **Quotation/Conversation:** She replied, "Isn't that extraordinary!"
3. **3sss:** (three short staccato sentences for drama, with rhythm) [6,6,6; 5,4,3; 4,4,4; 3,3,3; 2,2,2; 4,3,2]

They came. They saw. They conquered. (2,2,2)
The Huns invaded Europe. They slaughtered everyone. None survived. (4,3,2)

4. **Simile or Metaphor:** (compares two unlike things or states one thing is something else)
   Simile: I love her like a sister.
   Metaphor: Her words are music to my ears.
5. **Dramatic Open and Close:** (A dramatic VSS that opens and closes a paragraph)
   The tornado turned. . . . Our town became matchsticks.
6. **Alliteration:** (Two or more words beginning with the same letter or letter blend sound)
   Clumsily, he **clawed** and **clambered** up the **cliff.**
   A **bevy** of **big, beautiful butterflies.**
7. **Triple Extensions:** (triple: word, phrase, clause repetitions, or repeating "ing" words, "ly" words, adjectives, or verbs)

   (word)

   Fearing for his sheep, **fearing** the town's people would not respond, and **fearing** for his life, Peter screamed, "Help!"

   (adverb clause)

   They lived in a land **where** the winter was harsh, **where** food became scarce, and **where** provisions had to be stored.

   ("ing" words)

   Begging, pleading, and **whining** will get you nowhere.

   (adjectives)

   The **patient, steadfast, nurturing** penguin guarded her nest.

   (verbs)

   With all his might, the mouse **gnawed, jerked,** and **yanked** at the thick rope.
8. **Cumulative sentence:** (base clause + modifying phrases—a . . . , "ing" word, "ed" word, "ly" word, to + verb, possessive pronouns: he, she, his, her, its)

   > She walked with measured steps, draped in striped and fringed cloths, treading the earth proudly, with a slight jingle and flash of barbarous ornaments. She carried her head high; her hair was done

> in the shape of a helmet; she had brass leggings to the knee, brass wire gauntlets to the elbow, a crimson spot on her tawny cheek, innumerable necklaces of glass beads on her neck; bizarre things, charms, gifts of witch men, that hung about her; glittered and trembled at every step. (Conrad, 1990, p. 55-6)

9. **Suspensive sentence:** (a cumulative sentence that suspends the base clause until the end)

    > Rubbing his hands together, running his hungry eyes over the steaming food, anticipating the feast, savoring its aromas, stunned by his good fortune, realizing an opportunity like this may never come again, he sat down. (Landon, 2008, p. 64)

10. **Balanced sentence:** (hinges in the middle; paralleling or altering key words)
    It was the best of times; it was the worst of times.

(Adapted from Pudewa, 2015; Landon, 2008.)

Learning the forms, phrases, and clauses that make up sentences, and understanding the different ways these elements may be creatively manipulated helps writers to create sentences and paragraphs with an interesting variety of structure and style. Through a careful study of these advanced techniques, writers of all ages may improve their writing skills.

7

Sheltered Instruction for Writing

This sentence-level writing intervention outlines the language objective for this writing method, but like sheltered instruction, a strategy used for teaching English language learners, our writing approach has dual objectives: one for language and one for content. For the language objective, the goal is to explicitly teach the craft of sentence construction. A convenient way to teach the mechanics of sentence structure and style is through the use of informational text. Therefore, the academic content for guided practice uses grade-level content objectives required by the state.

The content objective for this writing intervention is to horizontally differentiate academic content learning to meet the needs of all intelligences and learning styles. To accommodate for the neurodiversity of young learners, content is supported through a variety of multisensory learning activities. A cognitively differentiated writing model uses social science and science topics to teach a sentence-level writing intervention, and academic content learning is taught through eight distinct modalities. The goal of cognitively differentiated instruction is to add breadth to how content is presented to students and to deliver lessons in all the languages of learning.

Most elementary teachers use cognitively differentiated activities. When teachers support a topic through movies, song, art, graphic organizers, artifacts, role-play, journal reflections, partner work, or hands-on experiential activities, they horizontally differentiate for the different ways that students learn. This writing model is simply more intentional about including cognitively differentiated instruction.

Seasoned teachers may be asking, "Is cognitively differentiated instruction the same as multisensory learning?" The answer is both yes and no. *Multisensory learning* means so many different things to people, depending on who is using the term. Some people think that *multisensory learning* means **adding** music, art, and physical education to the school day. Cognitively differentiated learning means to teach content **through** music, art, and physical movement. Because some students' learning languages are arts-based, cognitively differentiated lessons include arts-integrated instruction.

In the example of the "turtle" write, a cognitively differentiated lesson might include a learning song, chant, or poem that the students rehearse. Learning may be supported by a movie or beautifully illustrated "read alouds" and the teacher may have the students draw, label, and color a picture of a turtle. She may also choose to bring a turtle into the classroom as a natural artifact for students to examine and to teach about its care. Many multimodal activities are built into this writing method, such as oral retelling, oral guided practice, graphic organizers, partner work, journal reflections, and presentations.

Seasoned teachers may have noticed that the pedagogical pendulum of practice is swinging back toward a focused emphasis on skills acquisition, yet the latest adoptions for math and reading are heavy with arts-integrated activities as well. Math is graphic, visual, and hands-on, and reading curricula come with colorful illustrated song charts for the classroom. The latest trends in curricula development reflect an emphasis on skills-based instruction using a multimodal approach; this trend motivates us to want to explore the science behind this shift in pedagogy.

In Part II of our elementary writing model, we want to examine studies in educational neuroscience and cognitive psychology to develop a rationale for cognitively differentiated content learning using an arts-integrated approach. Through a study of the educational neuroscience behind arts-integrated learning, we seek to provide educators a rationale that explains how cognitively differentiated activities affect learning and memory. We endeavor to establish the cognitive benefits of arts-integrated instruction based on the way the brain learns. Our research supports the shift we see in educational pedagogy—that the most effective instruction is skills-based and multisensory.

II

CONTENT OBJECTIVE
Cognitively Differentiated Learning

What is cognitively differentiated learning?

8

Cognitively Differentiated Learning

The human brain is a little understood organ that receives and sends multisensory information (Johansson, 2008; Olsen, 1995). The brain is also a multiprocessing marvel. External sensory input is received from the spinal cord and relayed to the limbic system, which redistributes the information down multiple pathways to various regions in the cerebral cortex for processing and analysis. Whatever information the cortical processing systems deem relevant and meaningful is sent back to the limbic system for long-term memory storage and later use (Olsen, 1995).

Howard Gardner (1999) defined intelligence as "a biopsychological potential to process information that can be activated in a cultural setting to solve problems or create products that are of value in a culture" (p. 14). Or one could say that a person's intellectual disposition for knowing and learning depends on which cortical processing systems have the most natural potential to activate. This physiological potential defines our intelligence. How we learn best circumscribes the cognitive processing systems that are most natural to our ability to learn.

The human brain receives information through multiple sensory modalities. Dr. Sousa (2011a), an educational neuroscience consultant, notes, "The brain is a parallel processor and deals with many items simultaneously" (p. 60); it retains only the information that the multifunctional, multidimensional brain determines is relevant and meaningful.

Neuroscientists are only beginning to unlock and understand some of the brain's mysteries, thanks to new neuroimaging techniques, especially the groundbreaking imaging technology using positron emission tomography (PET) and functional magnetic resonance imaging (fMRI). From the explosion of information about the brain, a new breed of science has been born:

educational neuroscience. This new science sparks an investigation into new rationales for learning, and it informs the philosophy behind our sentence-level writing intervention and cognitively differentiated writing model.

While many elementary teachers recognize the importance of supporting learning through multisensory activities, some readers may ask, "Why is it important to teach academic content through song, movement, and art?" For those who may question the value of multimodal learning, this research-based investigation seeks to provide a rational response based on scientific studies. Over the past thirty years, many studies have demonstrated the value of arts-based instruction to enhance academic achievement, motivation, and performance. Most educators would not argue that instruction in the arts enriches one's life, and that it is an important part in the education of the whole child.

During our childhood, our parents gave us lessons in piano, gymnastics, and trampoline. Our father taught us how to play guitar, sing, and yodel in harmony. He taught us how to jitterbug, ski, cliff dive, draw, ride a horse bareback, and play tag on a steep mountaintop shale slide. These experiences absolutely enriched our lives and heavily influenced our teaching style. Our cognitively differentiated writing model uses artful, active experiences as teaching strategies to enrich student learning and to reach those learners who otherwise struggle within traditional classrooms.

If we want to create a fair learning environment for all, then we need to better understand cognitively differentiated learning. Most of us probably recognize that when it comes to how information is presented, we have strengths and weaknesses as to how well we learn. Eulalie has difficulty remembering information delivered orally. She needs to see content written down; an even more effective presentation allows her to see it and do it. Leta, on the other hand, loves lectures. She remembers almost everything she hears. For her, the challenge has been assimilating meaning through text. She often has to reread passages to comprehend what is written. For both of us, if we learn anything through song, we can recall that information verbatim. Each brain processes information differently depending on individual dispositions of knowing and learning.

In his book *How the Brain Learns,* Dr. Sousa (2011a) states, "Experienced teachers have recognized for years that students learn in different ways" (p. 58). Although the whole subject of learning preferences remains the subject of much debate, there is little argument that people have various internal and environmental preferences when they are learning (p. 60). Leta and Eulalie are twins. They are alike in many ways. However, when it comes to how they learn, they have almost nothing in common. Experienced teachers understand this phenomenon and try to accommodate the various ways students know and learn.

Cognitively differentiated learning strives to present lessons in as many sensory modalities as possible. As we discussed, simply adding music, art, and physical education to the school day does not constitute multimodal, brain-based learning. Cognitively differentiated learning uses a variety of symbol-processing systems to present academic information through modalities that are natural to the brain's ability to learn. Because several of the brain's processing systems are creative in nature, cognitively differentiated learning uses the arts as a teaching methodology throughout curricula. Our investigation explores scientific studies that offer novel insights on the cognitive merit of teaching academics through the creative modalities.

Our hope is that this investigation into the effect of active, arts-based experiences on academic achievement could inspire more left-brain (logical/analytical) educators to consider incorporating more right-brain (creative/intuitive) strategies. It seems that left-brain thinkers are the ones most drawn to administration. Their particular set of talents is what makes them so good at what they do. Yet the majority of students are actually right-brain oriented. It is easy to convince a creative/intuitive learner of the value of multimodal learning, whereas achieving buy-in from logical, analytical thinkers is a tougher sell. Through a logical and analytical presentation of statistical data on the effectiveness of cognitively differentiated instruction, we hope that left-brain thinkers will be intellectually persuaded of its educational value.

Why should we teach academic content through arts-integrated experiences?

9

Rationale

Teaching through the Arts

> Human nature is not a machine to be built after a model,
> and set to do exactly the work prescribed for it,
> but a tree, which requires to grow and develop itself on all sides,
> according to the tendency of the inward forces which make it a living thing.
>
> —John Stuart Mill, 1859, in R. T. Tripp, 1970, p. 174

One of the things that makes us human is our ability to create and appreciate art. The greatest art is that motivated by the attempt to express the ineffable spirit. The artist, more than anyone, recognizes the aesthetic *sui generis* quality of human personality, as well as understands the artistic impulse and drive to create novel works and ideas. Through art, "thought can merge wholly into feeling and feeling can merge wholly into thought" (Thomas Mann, 1913, in R. T. Tripp, 1970, p. 36). Through art there is no limit to vision, no restriction of domain, and no borders for the imagination. Because art is an expression from the mind of humans, art is a living thing.

It follows that the human brain is animated—not a device made of wheels and gears, but more like a tree that "grows and develops on all sides." Because all knowledge must pass through the sensory processing systems of our brain, that means learning is a dynamic process. The temperament of each individual is neurally distinct, driven by its own unique inward forces, and this disposition determines how we feel, see, perceive, interpret, and experience life. These forces influence how we learn.

For high-sensory, intuitive learners, artistic experiences not only define their learning style, but to "grow and develop on all sides" these students require rich, arts-integrated instruction to best comprehend and retain their lessons. So once again, the reader may be wondering, "Are there logical, research-based reasons within the realm of science that support teaching academics through active arts-integrated experiences?"

A rationale for arts-integrated learning can be found in research from neuroscience and cognitive psychology. Across the breadth of our teaching careers, we have held a fascination and curiosity for how the brain learns in an attempt to better understand the neurodiversity of young learners. Various studies coupled with student observations motivated the development of a multisensory writing model; it compelled us to differentiate our teaching strategies and to design interventions that help serve individual student learning needs in a seemingly "one-size-fits-all" educational system (Burnaford, Brown, Doherty, & McLaughlin, 2007; Gazzaniga, 2008; Ginns, 2005; Melnick, Witmer, & Strickland, 2011).

Art advocates and creative, intuitive educators have been struggling to provide strong cognitive arguments for why kindergarten through twelfth grade curricula should include dedicated time for arts instruction. Many parents, day care providers, and educators agree that training in the artistic disciplines is essential to the development of the whole child. Some have argued that knowledge and skills acquired through the arts transfer to nonart domains (Gazzaniga, 2008). Others argue that an arts-based education promotes motivation and engagement, improves school attendance, and enhances academic achievement (Melnick, Witmer, & Strickland, 2011; Smithrim & Upitis, 2005; Young, 2010).

While many have elaborated on the potential advantages offered through the arts, several neuroscience educators from Johns Hopkins University noticed that the most distinctive cognitive benefit has been continually overlooked—namely, that "utilizing artistic activities for instruction in other content areas may be a particularly effective means of enhancing long-term retention of content" (Rinne, Gregory, Yarmolinskaya, & Hardiman, 2011).

ART AND COGNITION

Art educator and scholar Arthur Efland (2002) explained the cognitive aspect of learning found in the arts and attempted to debunk the persistent perception that the arts impart affective and aesthetic value, but possess minimal cognitive merit. The assumption he strives to dispel is that the arts are intellectually inferior modes of knowing and learning, an entrenched mindset proposed and purported since the time of Plato.

Platonic ideals extolled the virtues of logical thinking and placed it higher in status than sensory knowledge, which was thought to be fraught with distortion and misperception. Yet because the realm of the abstract is difficult for the average person to grasp, parents and educators rely on sensory aids to make abstract concepts more concrete. They realize that models, maps, diagrams, graphic organizers, pictures, movies, songs, stories, actions, drama, and hands-on experiential projects are modalities that help make learning more comprehensible and understandable.

A bias against the arts seems to be deeply ingrained in science, psychology, and educational pedagogy (Efland, 2002; Sperry, 1973). Experimental psychologists borrowed their model of research from the natural sciences, which purport that every observable effect has a cause, and applied this principle to human behavior. The problem with such a view is that human behavior cannot be predicted, nor can it be reduced to zeros, ones, and twos. This reverence for scientific forms of understanding relegated other forms of knowing and learning as inconsequential. Efland's mission was to describe the educative role of the arts within a cognitive perspective as valuable to the educational experience of the whole child. He observed and offered an integrated view of three contending philosophies of cognition.

1. That the mind is a computational function using symbols
2. That cognition is a constructive process used to enable individuals to secure meaning
3. That learning includes the acquisition of social reality; that learning becomes meaningful when it occurs in a sociocultural or situational context (Efland, 2002, p. 156)

Secondly, Efland (2002) noted that the Western worldview contained "strong philosophical dualisms which worked to separate mind from body, cognitive from affective, real from imaginative, and science from art" (p. 156). Many of the great theorists in education, like Piaget and Bloom, perpetuated the age-old dichotomy, placing the sciences in the cognitive domain, while the arts were relegated to a noncognitive category. Consequently, school curricula and administrative decisions typically reflect a minor status for the arts.

Efland reports that the 1950s ushered in the cognitive revolution. Following suit, educational philosophy shifted focus from the behavior of the learner (behaviorism) to the learner's way of constructing knowledge (constructivism) to the idea that schemata, images, and concepts are symbolic entities or systems created by the mind to represent reality and that the accumulation of these symbolic structures represents learning (Efland, 2002).

In 1967, Nelson Goodman at Harvard University proposed and directed a research study called Project Zero—an investigation into the construction of meaning through various symbol-processing systems. Goodman's (1978) research was instrumental in leading to the development of Gardner's multiple intelligence (MI) theory. In the early 1990s, Gardner defined MI theory as describing differing domains of knowledge that have different symbol-processing systems, each one representing a different intelligence. Basically, Goodman's ideas, Piaget's symbol-processing orientation, and Vygotsky's sociocultural perspectives evolved into Gardner's "frames of mind" (Efland, 2002).

Efland (2002) summarized Goodman's philosophical perspective that each symbol-processing system has cognitive and emotional components.

> In establishing that the arts constituted distinct kinds of symbol systems, Goodman argued that they had an essentially cognitive function in human life.... A persistent critic of the epistemological tradition inherited from Descartes and Locke, Goodman argued that experience of works of art is not a matter of passive reception, but rather one of active inquiry. Unlike epistemologists who distinguished between science and art on the basis of a difference between cognition and emotion, Goodman argued that perception, cognition, and emotions are involved in both domains, that emotion itself, has a cognitive component. The symbol systems of art, like those of science, are used in constructing different versions of the world, and none of these systems can be reduced to another. (p. 60)

Efland (2002) also credits Michael Parsons (1992), who charted children's developmental stages for understanding art, for noting that how we perceive information and learn best is somewhat analogous to learning a language.

The research program of Project Zero was largely indebted to Goodman's idea that each art medium is a symbol system in its own right, being in some way analogous to a natural language. This idea contributed to the recognition of the arts as cognitive areas, each operating with discrete symbol systems. Indeed, MI theory greatly extended the categories of cognitive activity that general education should strive to cultivate. Recognizing that schools favor the cultivation of logical-mathematical and linguistic intelligence at the expense of the other intelligences, Gardner has steadfastly advocated that schools dedicate more time to the intelligences typically neglected in public schools (Efland, 2002, p. 61).

Efland (2002) recognized that in order for the arts to gain merit within the cognitive domain, they must provide cognitive benefits that other subjects do not. In particular, he wondered what special cognitive operations and strategies the arts can offer that will distinguish them from other domains of learning. While Efland presents several arguments for the cognitive value of the arts—(1) they help to integrate knowledge, (2) they stimulate imagination, and (3) they have aesthetic value—he overlooks the most distinctive argument: that teaching through the arts may enhance long-term memory of other content areas.

10

Arts-Integrated Learning

In an article published in *Mind, Brain, and Education,* Rinne, Gregory, Yarmolinskaya, and Hardiman (2011) present a seminal work explaining why arts integration—the use of the arts as a methodology throughout curriculum—may improve long-term retention of academic content. They review a variety of long-term memory effects well known in cognitive psychology and argue that arts integration naturally takes advantage of these memory effects.

Rinne and associates (2011) present neurologically sound evidence for how the arts contain discrete cognitive capabilities, which make them a powerful teaching tool and effective delivery system for academic content. When one uses multiple symbol systems to learn and process information, it stimulates multiple memory pathways throughout multiple areas of the brain. Students who rehearse academic content through song, chant, movement, drama, creative writing, and art-based, hands-on projects generate multimodal memory traces leveraging a number of special memory effects that positively influence the brain's ability to retain content.

Rinne and partners' (2011) research helped define the neuroscience behind this sentence-level writing intervention and cognitively differentiated writing model. Our multimodal strategies and techniques evolved over twenty years of practice in the classroom and we credit the success of our arts-integrated methods to the use of these unique memory effects, which are deeply embedded throughout this writing intervention.

Rinne and associates (2011) review eight memory effects that have been well documented over the last twenty to thirty years and show how each one is naturally incorporated into one or more forms of artistic activity. We demonstrate the ways that this writing model capitalizes on each of the following memory effects:

1. Rehearsal
2. Elaboration
3. Generation
4. Enactment
5. Oral production
6. Effort after meaning
7. Emotional arousal
8. Pictorial representation

REHEARSAL EFFECT

It may seem obvious to say that repeated rehearsal of information affects subsequent recall of that information. In 1971 Rundus conducted research that undeniably demonstrated that repeated, spaced rehearsals increased recall ability. Craik and Watkins (1973) observed that for rehearsal to be effective, it needs to be elaborative, or tie new information to prior knowledge. Rehearsal that establishes a more elaborate memory trace is more likely to be remembered. Rinne and colleagues (2011) noted, "Artistic activity may offer a more effective way to prompt elaborative rehearsal, as students will likely be more motivated to engage in artistic activities than to simply repeat after the teacher" (p. 90).

Table 10.1 lists the arts-integrated rehearsal opportunities to support the content objectives of the sentence-level writing intervention embedded within our elementary writing model.

Table 10.1. Arts-Integrated Rehearsal Opportunities

Art-Integrated Activity	Minimum Rehearsals
Learning song	20
Actions with song	20
Shared read aloud (text summary)	1
Generate propositions	1
Key Word Outline (create, retell, write)	3
Generate writing matrix	1
Write rough draft	1
Peer edit	1
Write final draft	1
Art project	1
Speech	15
Presentation practice	10
Semester presentation	3

For example, to learn a new learning song, students would probably practice a minimum of ten times. During practice for the presentation, they would practice that same song, again, probably a minimum of ten times. So the minimal rehearsal opportunities for practicing one learning song would be twenty repetitions.

Arts integration, which is the essence of this cognitively differentiated writing model, naturally provides ample opportunities to embed repeated, spaced rehearsals of grade-level content matter into the writing workshop through creative activities that are engaging, meaningful, and fun.

ELABORATION EFFECT

As mentioned in the previous section, if one links new information to prior knowledge, it can improve memory retention. Anderson and Reder (1979) argue that an increase in the quantity and richness of semantic elaborations creates another level of processing, adding a layer of complexity called "depth of processing." They maintained, "Because extent of elaboration is the critical variable, a better spatial metaphor for the 'depth of processing' phenomenon might be 'breadth of processing,'" arguing that long-term memory is the result of a number of elaborations across multiple domains (p. 385).

Craik and Lockhart (1972) reported that memory can be classified into three levels of storage: sensory stores, short-term memory, and long-term memory; it is widely accepted that a series or hierarchy of processing stages exists. Their work demonstrated that only deeper processing will lead to an improvement in memory.

Hiroshi Toyota (2010) observed that self-generated and self-corrected elaboration led to better recall than experimenter-provided elaboration. For instance, a target word "baby" may be an incongruous word in the context (e.g., "_____ drinks beer"), but would be congruous in another context (e.g., "_____ drinks milk"). Having to generate or correct a target word facilitates better recall than when the experimenter provides one. If one is asked to draw elaborate inferences while one reads (Reder, 1979) or elaborately relate new information to one's self in some way (Klein & Kihlstrom, 1986), then elaboration creates a stronger memory trace. Rinne and colleagues (2011) offer the following comments:

> A wide variety of artistic activities seem to naturally involve the kind of elaboration that is likely to improve subsequent recall of material. Activities in which students are asked to write stories that incorporate information to be remembered will naturally lead to elaboration of the information provided. So, too, it seems that writing a poem or song or creating a work of visual art may

often require students to elaborate and create a background context that would be absent if information were considered in isolation. The process of creating a surrounding context contributes to the establishment of a more elaborate memory trace. (p. 91)

In our writing intervention, students are asked to express what they already know about a topic. During the read aloud, students are encouraged to sketch key ideas and record personal connections, either through drawings or note taking. As students write, they are encouraged to imagine themselves in the scene. Through their art projects, students are invited to elaborate and create their version of what they have learned. Students are encouraged to express their learning through the following presentations: oration, drama, movement, dance, song, and arts-based authentic projects and props. The arts provide a vehicle for elaborative rehearsal that is distinctive and memorable.

GENERATION EFFECT

Another well-known effect on memory is the *generation effect,* which means that generating a response leads to better retention than if one is simply told or reads the information (Jacoby, 1978; Slamecka & Graf, 1978). A wide variety of explanations for the generation effect have been offered, and Bertsch, Pesta, Wiscott, and McDaniel (2007) provide a thorough summary of these in their metaanalytic review, which examines over eighty-six studies. In 2008, McDaniel and Bugg argued that information that has been generated by the person is more unusual or distinctive than information that is read. Kinjo and Snodgrass (2000) also found a strong generation effect for pictures. Rinne and associates (2011) state:

> Regardless of what causes the generation effect, knowledge that generation of information improves recall would clearly be useful to teachers in a classroom setting. When possible, teachers might engage students in activities through which they generate information instead of simply receiving it in written or oral form. (p. 91)

The sentence-level writing intervention relies heavily on student generated activities, such as:

- Sketching or drawing key ideas or taking notes during the "read aloud"
- Generating propositions from sketches or notes
- Generating the contentives (key words) in the text

- Generating a Key Word Outline
- Oral retelling—summarizing from a Key Word Outline
- Brainstorming forms, phrases, and clausals and recording them in the Writing Matrix
- Generating a written summary
- Editing and revising
- Generating an art project that supports the learning
- Preparing speeches
- Performing a presentation or celebration of learning

Asking students to generate the information they need makes the content more distinctive and unusual. Creative activities are memorable for this very reason. The methodology behind the cognitively differentiated writing model is that most learning is student-generated, and academic content is rehearsed through a variety of creative activities.

ENACTMENT EFFECT

According to Rinne and partners (2011), "The enactment effect refers to the finding that physically acting out material leads to improved recall relative to simply reading or hearing the material" (pp. 91–92). It has been repeatedly shown that a list of phrases such as "to jump rope" is recalled better if the subjects are asked to perform the action than if they only listen to them (Cohen, 1983; Mohr, Engelkamp, & Zimmer, 1989). The researchers explained that self-performed acts create a motor memory encoding, as well as verbal and imaginal encoding, producing recall superiority.

In 2000, Ann Podlozny conducted a metaanalysis of studies on the use of drama in the classroom to investigate the relationship between drama instruction and various kinds of academic achievement. Her results demonstrated that enactment promotes deeper learning in a variety of verbal domains. Podlozny (2000) concluded, "Clearly, drama is an effective tool for increasing achievement in story understanding, reading achievement, reading readiness, and writing" (p. 268).

Using the memory effect for enactment, the cognitively differentiated writing model strives to put movement, actions, or dance to as many learning songs as possible. We have also noticed that many children naturally want to generate movement to music. Retelling or summarizing through enactment using games such as Charades is another way to appropriate this memory effect and to strengthen memory traces through motor encoding.

The enactment effect is one reason this writing model is committed to regular celebrations of learning (Cambourne, 1998). Orchestrating semester presentations provides a variety of enactment opportunities to practice content learning, and it thoroughly capitalizes on the powerful memory effects of rehearsal, elaboration, generation, and enactment.

PRODUCTION EFFECT

According to MacLeod, Gopie, Hourihan, Neary, and Ozubko (2010), a recently discovered effect that closely parallels those previously mentioned is the production effect: "producing a word aloud during study, relative to simply reading a word silently, improves explicit memory" (p. 671). In a following study, Ozubko and MacLeod (2010) proposed that oral production of a word improves memory because it makes the information more distinctive relative to just reading it. They concluded that:

> The production effect may therefore prove to be a useful technique in study situations, or whenever relatively quick and easy memory enhancement is desired. As noted earlier, the existence of the production effect fits the common notion that information studied aloud is better remembered. (p. 1546)

Rinne and associates (2011) suggest that:

> Finding ways to take advantage of the production effect via arts integration is a relatively straightforward task; when students sing songs or engage in theatrical performances that include information to be remembered, they will produce that information orally, promoting retention. (p. 92)

Embedded within our writing intervention are a myriad of opportunities to orally generate, produce, and practice content information. Daily, students orally produce academic learning through song. Weekly, students generate and orally produce summary propositions, forms, phrases, clauses, Key Word Outlines, and summaries, as well as share their own writings with a friend or in front of the class.

Each semester students produce a presentation for family and friends. Presentation is a powerful teaching tool because it requires a multitude of elaborate multimodal rehearsals, establishing a breadth of multimodal memory traces. Arts integration is a vibrant way to orally produce and practice content from grade-level standards through mediums that are neither redundant nor boring.

EFFORT AFTER MEANING EFFECT

The phrase "effort after meaning" was coined by British psychologist Frederic Bartlett (1932; cited in Rinne et al., 2011, p. 92). He proposed a direct relationship between the processes involved in comprehension and acts of remembering—that when one has to exert effort to understand, perceive, reason, or comprehend, that information is easier to recall.

Auble and Franks (1978, 1979) found when one has to exert effort toward comprehension, the process involves greater elaboration or deeper processing and the subsequent "aha" experience produces significantly greater recall. In a more recent study, Zaromb and Roediger (2009) found the effort after meaning paradigm—which is similar to the generation, enactment, and production paradigms in that exerting effort to understand content may make the information more distinctive or unusual—may lead to a deeper processing of the information.

The "effort after meaning" effect is the neuroscience that explains why student-generated processes, such as brainstorming, are so essential to learning. In our writing intervention, students have to generate specific elements for their compositions. In the early stages of the writing method, brainstorming is a group effort. Rather than the teacher providing the essential elements needed for writing, the class must generate a variety of examples for each category, corporately modeling a higher level of achievement than may be attained by any one individual student.

For the novice, it is generally easier to add to or bounce off the thoughts of others than to generate a variety of ideas from within the solitary confines of one's own mind. As students work in a group to generate a variety of elements with which to write, the effort they must exert helps to expand their lexicon of syntactical resources and enhance their brain's ability to retain that information.

EMOTIONAL AROUSAL EFFECT

It has long been recognized that our emotional memories are often the most permanent—that high levels of emotional arousal facilitate a powerful memory trace. Brown and Kulick (1977) describe this phenomenon as "flashbulb memories." A perfect example of the strength of emotional memories is that most Americans can recall with amazing clarity where they were and what they were doing when the Twin Towers were destroyed in the terrorist attack on September 11, 2001.

Another example one can use to personally test the strength of emotional memory is to ask the reader if he or she can recall most of the words to the math song *O Isosceles,* which will be introduced in chapter 15. Because a Christmas song produces a strong emotional response, the reader may be able to remember the words to the song, even though he or she has read it only once.

Cahill and McGaugh (1995) conducted experiments in which subjects read closely matched stories, with one being more emotionally neutral and the other more emotionally arousing. After testing retention two weeks later, they reported, "The results provide new evidence to support the contention that emotional arousal influences long-term memory in normal human subjects" (p. 410). In more recent investigations, McGaugh (2004) and Kensinger and Schacter (2008) found through brain imaging studies that the amygdala is involved in processing the consolidation of long-term memory. McGaugh (2004) explains:

> Emotionally significant experiences, whether pleasant or unpleasant, activate hormonal and brain systems that regulate the consolidation of newly acquired memories. Many neuromodulatory systems play a role, and critical interaction among them occur in the basolateral region of the amygdala. . . . Through the activation of these interacting systems our emotionally exciting experiences become well remembered. (p. 18)

Kensinger and Schacter (2008) added that during each memory phase of encoding, consolidation, and retrieval, "Limbic activity serves to modulate perceptual and mnemonic function to increase the likelihood that information is attended to, and that at least some details are retained" (p. 612).

This research provides neurobiological evidence as to why educators should strive to make learning emotionally exciting and engaging. Although worksheets and direct instruction have their place, they are not generally emotionally stimulating. They should be interspersed with activities that arouse the emotions. Again, this is why arts integration is so cognitively beneficial. Content remembered is content learned. The arts provide the modalities of learning that invite emotional expression, creativity, inquiry, ingenuity, intuitiveness, spontaneity, and passion; they integrate activities that arouse the emotions.

PICTURE SUPERIORITY EFFECT

The old adage "a picture is worth a thousand words" basically defines the picture superiority memory effect. It has been found in numerous studies (e.g., Hikari & Snodgrass, 2000; Mintzer & Snodgrass, 1999; Shepard, 1967) that information presented in the form of pictures is encoded in memory better than information presented in words. Defeyter, Russo, and McPartlin (2009) found that the picture superiority effect showed a clear developmental trend—that the effect is the most evident in school-age children and adults, while not as pronounced in younger children.

Gardner (1999) explains that the spatial intelligence learner learns through pictures the way the linguistic learner learns through words. For some learners, their natural learning language seems to prefer pictorial symbol processing. Teaching content through pictures also scaffolds English language learners and those with learning disabilities. For this reason our cognitively differentiated writing model intentionally integrates content using the following pictorial activities:

- Illustrated text and song charts
- Note-taking through drawings and sketches
- Retelling summaries practiced through graphic games, such as *Pictionary*
- Brainstorming choices visually recorded in a classroom-sized graphic or Writing Matrix
- Classroom-sized writing rubrics, checklists, and visuals
- Classroom visuals and charts organized in an aesthetically pleasing way
- Major grade-level content topics are supported through an art-based project
- Content learning is supported through movies and film documentaries
- Props and artifacts for the semester presentations generated by the students

Using a cognitively differentiated writing model, we strive to accommodate for a variety of symbol-processing systems, recognizing that students have different strengths. In all fairness, every student ought to be given opportunities to operate within his or her strengths, so hopefully everyone is given a chance to show off and to shine in the domains that are most natural to their ability to learn.

We conclude by reiterating that this sentence-level writing intervention uses and capitalizes on all the special memory effects. Arts-integrated instruction provides a pedagogical powerhouse of cognitive benefits that cannot be found in any other domains of learning. Content mastery requires long-term retention of vast amounts of information, and arts integration can help students and teachers reach that goal.

11

Arts-Integrated Instruction and Cognition

To answer Arthur Efland's (2002) question, "What cognitive abilities do the arts provide that other subjects cannot?" we respond in concert with Rinne, Gregory, Yarmolinskaya, and Hardiman (2011): "The use of the arts as a teaching methodology throughout curriculum has the cognitive ability to improve long-term retention of other academic content areas" (p. 89). By taking advantage of what neuroscientists and cognitive psychologists know about the eight special memory effects, our writing intervention teaches the craft of constructing sentences using a pedagogical model based on the idea that arts integration serves as a powerful tool for translating academic content into the natural learning languages of all learners.

Common Core State Standards, with their emphasis on standardized testing and increased accountability, have placed tremendous demands on students and teachers to master skills, content, and concepts, and to show adequate yearly progress. With the increased demands placed on students to retain content comes an increased responsibility on the part of teachers and administrators to use teaching techniques that fully appropriate the brain's learning and memory capacities, so students are offered every possible advantage when test time arrives.

Arts advocates may have noticed that we have not presented the traditional cognitive arguments for retaining the arts in schools. Although we agree that professional training in the artistic disciplines is essential to the development of the whole child, arts integration—using the arts as a teaching methodology—is not the same as dedicated classes in the arts. Teaching through the arts is a didactic technique used to support learning of grade-level content. We do recognize and acknowledge that a serious study of the arts may produce the following results:

- Studying a musical discipline builds a better brain; skilled musicians develop a thicker corpus callosum and show improved spatial-temporal reasoning, which may help with certain forms of math (Vaughn, 2000).
- Exercising regularly oxygenates and fuels the brain, allowing the brain to access more long-term memory areas (Fedewa & Ahn, 2011). David Sousa (2011), an educational consultant in educational neuroscience and prolific author, reports:

> Exercise was shown to be strongly correlated with increases in brain mass and cell production as well as in improved cognitive processing and mood regulation. These findings should encourage teachers to get students up and moving in their classrooms. It also should discourage administrators from eliminating recess and physical education classes, a common practice in the current era of high-stakes testing. (p. 15)

- Training in the visual arts cultivates the imaginative mind (Eisner, 2002), which will be an in-demand trait as we enter the conceptual age of the twenty-first century (Hardiman, 2010, p. 227; Pink, 2006, pp. 49–51).
- The transforming nature of the arts positively affects school culture, climate, and community (Catterall & Waldorf, 1999).
- Engaging in the arts enhances cultural understanding among diverse groups (Burstein & Knotts, 2010; Mandell & Wolf, 2003).
- Participating in the performing arts enhances verbal skills and reading achievement (Podlozny, 2000).

For a thorough exposition of the historical arguments supporting the arts, one may read the literature review by Burnaford, Brown, Doherty, and McLaughlin (2007).

In addition to all the phenomenal cognitive benefits that result from a serious study of the arts, there remains one contribution that propels the arts to the higher echelons of the cognitive domain, and that is their unique ability to facilitate learning and memory for other content areas. Eulalie relates a personal attestation for the cognitive value of arts-integrated instruction.

As Eulalie mentioned in her biography, she works as a private tutor for an international business couple. At the beginning of Eulalie's tutee's first grade year (2013), Eulalie introduced multiplication using her math intervention called, "Multiplication, Music, & Motion." She taught multiplication facts using a musical kinesthetic approach. By the end of the school year, Eulalie's tutee had all her multiples through twelve memorized, as well as their divisional equivalents. Presently, during the summer of 2014, her student has mastered her thirteens and fourteens. So, as we begin her second grade year, her tutee is ready to tackle her fifteens, and she is still only seven years old.

While Eulalie's student is an extremely bright and inquisitive child, she has some learning challenges, including dyslexia. Perhaps more children could learn at this rate given the same multisensory tool.

Early in our teaching careers we recognized that when students had a large body of information that needed to be memorized (e.g., the multiplication facts), if we put the content to song and movement, then students seemed to learn at a remarkable rate and they retained their lessons. Over and over again we have personally witnessed that arts-integrated learning seems to have the cognitive ability to enhance learning and memory for academic content.

WRITING: COGNITIVE AND PHYSICAL SKILLS

Neuroimaging studies are also helping educators to understand more about language development. While speaking is a natural human trait, reading and writing are not. Language results from an elaborate network of functions that include both hemispheres of the brain. For instance, when a child hears language spoken, he or she must process semantics, monitor for coherence, integrate text, interpret the perspective of the speaker, and process imaging of spatial information. Diane Williams (2010), an assistant professor in the Department of Speech-Language Pathology at Duquesne University, notes:

> Some children cannot listen to orally presented information and take notes at the same time—not because they are noncompliant, but because they have only enough cognitive resources to do one or the other. (p. 96)

Paul Dennison (2006), an authority on cognitive skills and reading achievement, states that reading is a physical activity as well as cognitive one. He lists the following physical activities that must happen simultaneously for reading to take place:

- Binocularity (using both eyes together in the visual field)
- Convergence (moving both eyes together to see something that's nearby)
- Tracking (moving both eyes together to cross the visual/auditory/kinesthetic midline for reading left to right)
- Sustained attention and concentration
- Directionality and motor planning
- Hearing and matching graphemes (symbols) and phonemes (speech sounds)
- Thinking (silent speech)
- Memory of sounds and shapes
- The visualization of letter patterns and word shapes

- Eye–hand coordination
- Timing, rhythm, and phrasing of speech pattern (Dennison, 2006, p. 27)

Dennison reiterates Williams's statements that reading and writing require a network of complex processing systems and consume a vast array of neural resources. The physical processing of sound (phonemes), visual symbols (graphemes), and fine motor movements (writing) involves a multitude of cognitive and physical skills.

Dennison and his wife Gail developed a learning support system called *Brain Gym* (2006). In theory, it connects learning to concrete, three-dimensional experiences by establishing and strengthening neural learning pathways in the three-dimensional body. In our own classrooms, we have observed the correlation between reading ability and the physical ability to perform cross-the-midline movement. Those students who frequently play games that include cross-lateral and cross-the-midline movement, like the clap-cross-clap partner songs and double-jump rope, seem to be the children who are good readers. And those students who struggle doing movements like opposite-elbow-to-opposite-knee are also, often, the students who struggle with learning to read.

Observing this connection motivated us to incorporate as much cross-the-midline movement with our learning songs as possible, hoping that by strengthening the three-dimensional neural networks necessary to do motor movements, we will also enhance the neural resources needed for reading. This correlation is one that bears further investigation.

Williams (2010) also observed gender differences in language processing. Williams cites a study by Burman, Bitan, and Booth (2008) in which the researchers' investigation suggested that boys do not convert sensory information to language as easily as girls. From her research, Williams concludes:

> Like athletic skills, spoken-language skills are determined by a child's genetic makeup and the amount of time and effort spent on practice and development of the skills. Not all children are capable of the same level of verbal expression. Some children are slower processors and some are faster processors of language. Therefore, some children may be verbally fluent while others struggle to put their thoughts into words. These differences are not related to innate intelligence or motivation; rather, they are related to individual differences in brain development. (p. 99)

One of Eulalie's most inspiring professors, Dr. Trish Lichau Shields, said something most insightful. After years of working with boys and observing how many agonized over verbally expressing themselves, Lichau Shields's judicious response was, "Give them the words they need." This sentence-level writing intervention strives to do exactly that. It scaffolds those students who are either slower verbal processors or who are learning English as a second language. The class brainstorming sessions use the strengths of those students who are strong verbal processors to support those students who struggle to find the words they need.

Because all the necessary elements needed for writing are posted on the board for everyone to see, those students who are verbally challenged are not relegated to face the obscurities of the blank page. We give students the words they need so no one needs to feel panicky or anxious because they cannot produce the necessary elements required. As students practice using a scaffold approach, the slower verbal processors are building a lexicon of forms, phrases, and clauses, so that eventually they will be able to find the words they need when they write.

COGNITIVELY DIFFERENTIATED TEACHING AND LEARNING

Of all the hats a teacher has to wear, one that comes naturally to most is "scientist." Teachers are forever asking questions, observing their surroundings, solving problems, collecting and organizing data, researching, recording, relating, reflecting, and nurturing and managing multifarious relationships. They are continually analyzing and synthesizing teaching and learning effectiveness; experimenting with innovative strategies and practices; striving to perfect the art, craft, and technique of their profession; zealously working toward the goal; and diligently pursuing the ultimate objective, the one immutable goal: student success.

Analyzing and understanding the teaching and learning relationship gives purpose and direction to our art. Science supports theory, theory inspires philosophy, philosophy determines pedagogy, pedagogy forms structure, structure circumscribes content, content directs goals, goals demand strategies, strategies exact method, and method should differentiate for different ways of thinking and processing information.

Neuroscience supports the theory that people have different dispositions of knowing and learning. Multiple intelligence (MI) theory inspires the teaching philosophy that learning is most effective when lessons are delivered via multiple symbol-processing systems. A multisensory philosophy determines that our pedagogy ought to accommodate for the neurodiversity of all learners. An arts-integrated pedagogy forms the structure for a cognitively differentiated teaching model.

Because structure circumscribes whole-brain learning, content will be multisensory and arts-based. Teaching integrated content directs us to set goals that use the arts as a teaching methodology throughout curriculum so students will be able to understand and comprehend academic content in a language that is natural to their ability to learn. Attaining this goal demands cognitively differentiated strategies. A discrete plan exacts an explicit method. Whole-brain teaching techniques thoroughly differentiate for all dispositions of knowing and learning. Figures 11.1 and 11.2 graphically describe the Teaching and Learning Relationship and Cognitively Differentiated Writing Model.

Arts-integrated learning creates a marriage between academics and the arts. It generates symbiosis between science and art, theory and philosophy, and goals and method. The teaching and learning relationship may also describe the interrelatedness of the learning process between academics and the arts. While our diagram shows a two-dimensional plane, the teaching and learning relationship is more accurately a three-dimensional sphere, because elements also interrelate across the plane.

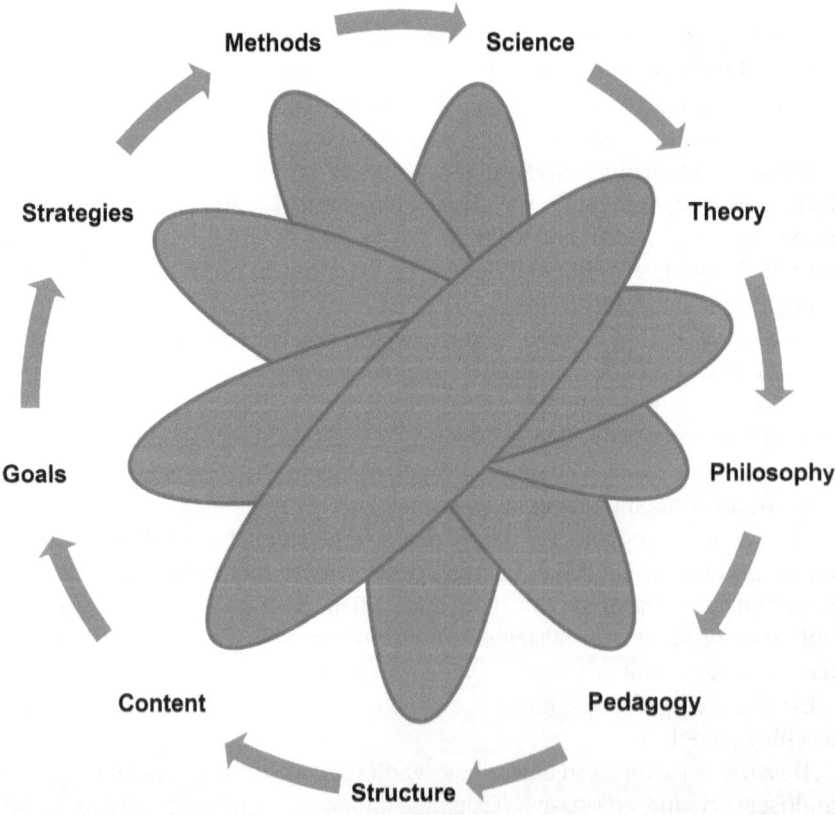

Figure 11.1. Teaching & Learning Relationship

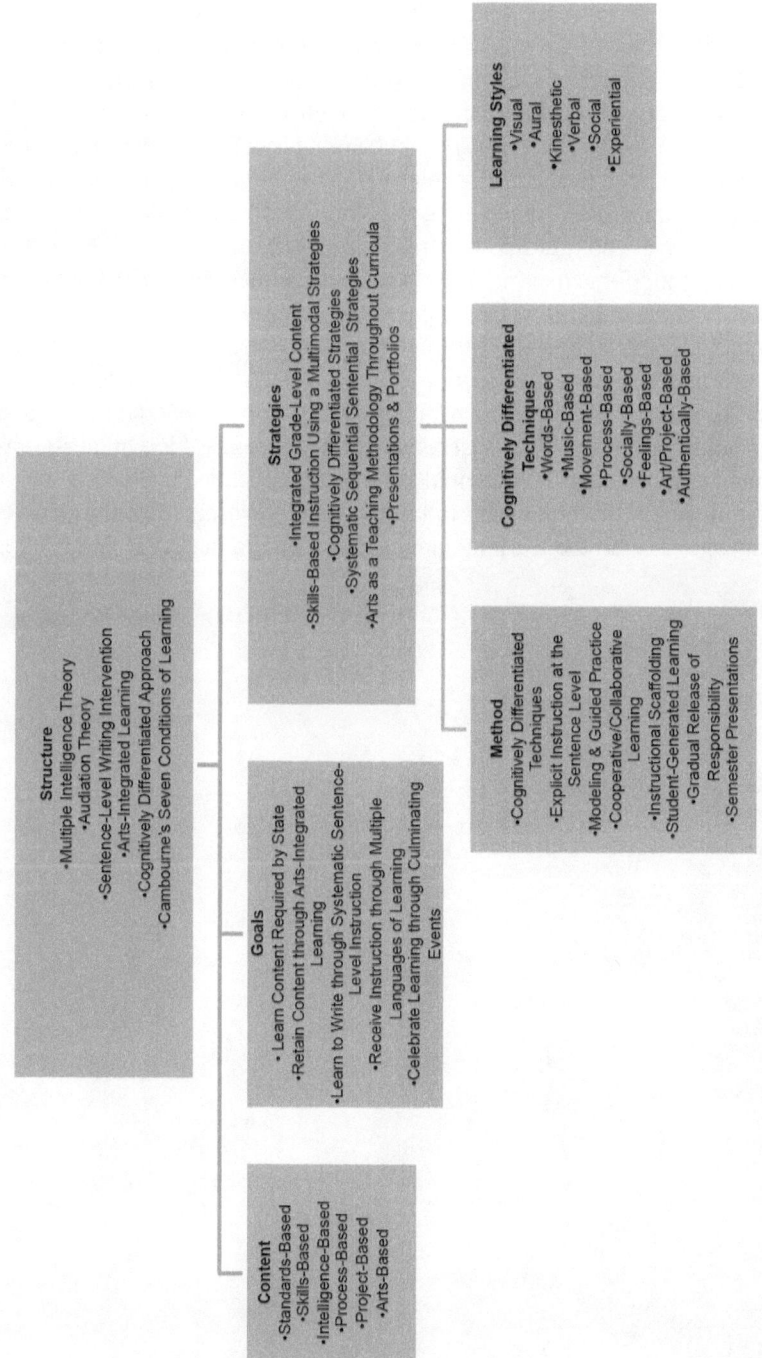

Figure 11.2. A Cognitively Differentiated Writing Model

For example, MI science substantiates that arts-integrated instruction provides an effective tool for retaining and remembering academic information. This relates to the art of teaching because it determines that our pedagogy includes delivery of academic content through the creative modalities. MI theory is supported by the axiology that learning requires differentiated strategies, which relates to the philosophy behind an arts-integrated cognitively differentiated approach. Academic goals state the educational objectives one hopes to achieve, and multimodal strategies and techniques provide the most effective method for achieving those goals. Academics and the arts are quintessential companions in the teaching and learning relationship.

Cognitively differentiated learning integrally supports the teaching and learning relationship. It also works to unite western educational pedagogy with cross-cultural pedagogy by using culturally responsive techniques, such as cooperative-based, project-based, and community-based learning. An arts-integrated approach has the potential to integrate educational worldviews, yet it accommodates individual ways of knowing and learning. It speaks a universal language, as well the learning languages unique to human understanding.

Why should we teach academic content through song?

12

Song as a Teaching Tool

Our Land Is Portland

(Sung to the tune: "You Are My Sunshine")
Text: Eulalie Hatfield

Our land is Portland, it's such a rich land
The land of osprey and the Great Blue Heron
With rivers of steelhead, Chinook, and salmon
Portland, the land that we love

Portland's between two mighty rivers
The great Columbia and the Willamette
They formed a low land, the Willamette Valley
Portland, the land that we love

Portland's between two mountain ranges
One is volcanic, namely the Cascades
One's due to earthquakes, it's called the Coast Range
Portland, the land that we love

Hike Forest Park through mountain acres
Or ski Mount Hood when snow comes in winter
Or take a bike ride over miles of bike trails
Portland, the land that we love

We have the Timbers and the Trail Blazers
We have Powell's Book Store, River Place Marina
The Crystal Ballroom, the McMenamin Brothers
Portland, the land that we love

Song makes learning fun; it makes learning meaningful and memorable. Lyrics create an avenue that allows academics to be accessible to all learners. Music adds meaning to life. It speaks to the human experience and its many forms emotionally connect people to issues that are relevant to their existence. Lively melodies can arouse the spirit and spark imagination. Ballads touch the soul and often preserve one's memories in time. Some songs proclaim joy and celebration and directly invite one to dance. Song can stir one to action or reduce one to tears. Song is a powerful medium and it can also be a very effective teaching tool, as our study explores.

"Music, as a language, is a universal human trait" (Peretz, 2006, p. 1). It transcends culture, race, politics, and religion. Music has been around a long time. "Cave paintings depicting music go back 70,000 years. Flutes have been found in France dating as far back as 30,000 years ago" (Jensen, 2000, p. 19). Throughout history, song has been an expression of man's traditions, travails, and triumphs.

Song has chronicled civilizations and transmitted traditions. Much of what is known about the past has been learned because someone felt inspired to pass the knowledge down through song, chant, and oral storytelling. Many would argue that music is one of humanity's highest artistic achievements. In the words of the "poet laureate of medicine," Oliver Sacks (2007), "We are a musical species no less than a linguistic one" (p. xi). For most people, music matters.

For some, music defines how they learn. Some people learn best through images and pictures. They love movies, documentary programs, graphic novels, and illustrated texts. Still others need to experience learning through artful projects. They love designing, drawing, and constructing crafts and experimenting with color, line, and texture. Artists have a need to create and to make their own meaning. Doing and moving helps some to learn. For them, their whole body needs to express their ideas and feelings. They need action, like movement, dancing, touching, and hands-on experiences to interpret meaning.

Others have a need to express their reflections through words. These people love to create journals and diaries and to fill them with their thoughts, poetry, and musings. Writing helps them to make sense of their world. They write just because it feels good. Those who learn through music are drawn to musical productions; they notice musical scores in movies, they collect huge repertoires of their favorite artists, and they rarely forget the words to songs (Armstrong, 2000).

Many people, to a certain degree, are both artistic and musical learners. Most would rather do a science experiment than read about it. Beautifully illustrated text makes a topic more memorable. A diagram or a model helps clarify complex topics. Many people would rather memorize something through a song or a chant than by rote. For many, artful experiences enhance learning.

Mnemonic song is a creative way to combine these learning styles and roll them into one delivery system. Illustrated song charts create a visual experience, while melody is learned aurally. Producing melody and words is a kinesthetic activity, while the act of singing is experiential, verbal, and social. Song provides multimodal experiences for creating meaningful connections to a topic, which makes learning more memorable (Abbott, 2001).

Comprehension increases when students are allowed to rehearse content in a repetitive format that is not redundant or boring (Campabello, De Carlo, O'Neil, & Vacek, 2002). Mnemonic song can help students to remember their lessons and to retain the content teachers work so hard to teach (Rainey & Larsen, 2002; Peretz, Radeau, & Arguin, 2004). Song provides a powerful remediation tool, which supports both the learning disabled and English language learners (Gfeller, 1983; Li & Brand, 2009).

When teachers use musical mnemonics to teach core content, it enhances comprehension, improves memory retention, and helps to support the diverse learning needs of students. If educators differentiate instruction to include the creative intelligences, then the learning field is leveled, providing all learners a more equal opportunity for success. The purpose of our investigation is to study the effectiveness of mnemonic song for supporting learning and memory retention, and to demonstrate how musical mnemonics support the diverse range of learners in the elementary classroom.

BALANCED LEARNING THROUGH HORIZONTAL DIFFERENTIATION

Educators and neuroscientists agree that humans learn in a variety of ways (Armstrong, 2000; Gardner, 1999; Jensen, 2000; Sousa, 2010). Their theories state that the human brain processes information differently, depending on disposition of intelligence. Each intelligence has its own primary way of knowing, processing, and assimilating information—each learns best through a distinct modality. If there are different ways to learn, then there should be different ways to teach. When educators do not horizontally differentiate their instruction to accommodate for disposition of intelligence, we create an imbalance of learning.

Many artistic individuals (those who learn best through song, art, movement, and hands-on experiences) would agree that most academic instruction is not given in a modality that is natural to their ability to learn. Gardner has long argued that educators are not meeting the learning needs of all their students, but that curriculum and standardized tests are designed to favor only two of the intelligences: the linguistic learner and the logical-mathematical learner (Gardner, 1999).

As a rule, educators view the creative arts as separate from academic core, so it has not typically been considered an essential part of curriculum. This way of thinking produces a favorable learning environment for some, while marginalizing others. Creative learners may feel disadvantaged in traditional educational settings.

Educational theory and science inform teaching and learning strategies. *Best Practice: Today's Standard for Teaching and Learning in America* emphasized that methods need to be integrated, holistic, experiential, and expressive for learning to be meaningful and relevant for the child (Zemelman, Daniels, & Hyde, 2005). Through mnemonic songs, educators can integrate these progressive practices.

Song is a whole-brain activity that speaks in the language of each intelligence and meets every learning style. Song is memory drill made fun and with a lifelong benefit—one seldom forgets what one learns through song (Bartlett & Snelus, 1980). Song makes a content area accessible to most learners and improves memory retention. Educators may find song a useful tool in an era that demands more and more memorization skills from elementary students.

In this era of high-stakes testing, it is crucial that our students retain and comprehend their lessons. When funding and jobs hang on student performance, it becomes paramount that techniques that enhance the learning and remembering processes are found and implemented. Science, research, and educators have found that adding song to core curriculum will enhance academic gain (Campabello, De Carlo, O'Neil, & Vacek, 2002; Wallace, 1994).

Since the 1980s, reformers have tried to establish the value of including creative arts into classroom curriculum, believing that arts are essential to the development of the whole child. We believe that a more holistic approach to learning helps restore balance to instructional practices because it offers students more equitable access to academic content.

With such a high demand placed on students to meet AYP (adequate yearly progress), we must provide ample support for learners and learning styles. As teachers, we must not allow students to fail. According to William Glasser (1975), *schools* should not allow students to fail. If there are teaching tools that have been scientifically proven to enhance comprehension and improve memory retention, these should be in every classroom when appropriate.

Using a quantitative research analogy as an example, students are the receivers, the dependent variable. If many students are not learning, there appears to be an impediment in the transmission of knowledge. Although teachers are diligently teaching and students are trying hard, there appear to be too many students who cannot hear the transmission. Educators should not lay the cause of the problem on the backs of the dependent variables and blame the receivers. It is not always the students' fault that they do not comprehend and retain content; it could be there is a malfunction in the way that knowledge is communicated. In the words of Gardner (1999), "We are not the same; we do not all have the same kinds of minds; and education works most effectively if these differences are taken into account rather than denied or ignored" (p. 91).

When students struggle with assimilating and remembering core content, teachers call in specialists to work with the students' problems. To protect a child's self-esteem, educators could provide more effective tools for enhancing the learning and remembering processes. People learn differently. It is time to create a new paradigm for instructional practice. When lessons are presented in everyone's learning language, we offer all students equal access to academic content. Teaching through musical mnemonics is one way to create a balance of learning because it improves memory retention and it provides cognitively differentiated support for students (Li & Brand, 2009; Peynircioglu, Rabinovitz, & Tompson, 2008; Scruggs & Mastropieri, 2000; Wallace, 1994).

13

Operational Definitions

A *mnemonic* is defined as a tool to aid the memory. Using mnemonic songs to instruct core content gives students a tool to process information into their long-term memory so that it can be retrieved later when needed. Intelligence, as Gardner (1999) noted, is one's epistemological disposition of knowing and learning. Whole-brain learning theorists, like multiple intelligence theorists, believe that people's brains learn and retain information differently, depending on which dispositions are most dominant. They believe humans have aptitudes that are either logic–analytic dominant, or creative–intuitive dominant, and they further classify brain functions according to the aptitudes shown in table 13.1.

Cognition is "the mental action or process of acquiring knowledge and understanding through thought, experience, and the senses" (Oxford Dictionaries). *Cognitive differentiation* means instruction that is presented in

Table 13.1. Brain Function Aptitudes

Logic-dominant people are:	*Creative-dominant people are:*
Highly verbal	Not articulate (struggle with verbal expression of experiences)
Language-oriented	
Planned and structured	Highly developed sensory capacity
Sequential thinking	Simultaneous thinking
Time conscious	Feeling-, experience-oriented
All-or-none (outcome) oriented	Now-oriented
Technique-oriented	Flow- and movement-oriented
More focused on:	*More focused on:*
Sports (eye, hand, foot placement)	Sports (flow and movement)
Art (media, tool use, how to)	Art (image, emotion, flow)
Music (notes, beat, tempo)	Music (passion, rhythm, image)

the languages of each intelligence; synonymously, instruction is delivered in each learning style. To reach every intelligence, lessons should:

- Be presented logically, systematically, and methodically
- Be presented linguistically, through print
- Be illustrated through pictures, movies, diagrams, graphics, or visuals
- Be taught through song, chant, rhyme, or poetry
- Have a movement, dance, or physically active, hands-on component
- Include group work, partner work, and class discussion
- Have a reflection piece, either orally or written
- Connect to nature, artifacts, and living things in the environment (Armstrong, 2000, p. 22)

Instruction that includes the preceding elements enables lessons to be delivered in every learning style, which means they are delivered visually, aurally, kinesthetically, verbally, socially, and experientially. Cognitively differentiated lessons should be process-based, project-based, community-based, musically based, graphically based, cooperative, collaborative, holistic, and authentic, incorporating a full array of sensory experiences.

If teaching strategies take into account the propensities for learning aptitudes, intelligences, and learning styles, and use multisensory instructional activities for addressing all of these, then evidence suggests we can improve student learning and retention (Ginns, 2005). As one whole-brain educator stated simply, "When a teaching strategy works, it does so because it works with the way the brain learns" (Tyrer, 2002, p. 9).

RATIONALE: TEACHING CONTENT THROUGH SONG

Instructing through mnemonic song is a cognitively differentiated technique. Singing engages every learning style and it seems to be one of the most whole-brain activities one can do, according to Kimball (2010), who also posits:

> Memory appears to be enhanced by music because it involves the whole brain; when engaged with a song, the left brain (which handles language, logic, mathematics, etc.) processes the lyrics, while the right brain (which handles rhythm, rhyme, pictures, emotions, etc.) processes the music. (p. 317)

Because one learns a song by reading from a song chart, it is visual. When one hears the song and must discriminate melody and text, it is aural. Song is kinesthetic because the vocal cords, diaphragm, mouth, and tongue must work in synchrony to produce sound, pitch, words, and melody. If motions or dance are taught with the song, then it becomes extremely kinesthetic. Singing involves words, so song is verbal. It is social and experiential because singing is cooperative and requires active community participation.

Song speaks to every intelligence. By its very nature, song is logical; it has a predictable rhythm and tempo. Melody follows a pattern; it has method. The arrangement of choruses, verses, and phrases is systematic. Text of song is learned linguistically. Melody is learned musically. Illustrated song texts teach through pictures. Movement connects action to physical and visual imagery. The activity of singing is interpersonal because singing and movement require students to cooperatively work together to synchronize voice and motions. Singing can be intrapersonal. Because the words of songs tend to stay in one's memory, one tends to naturally reflect on the words as they roll in and out of one's mind. Song emotionally attaches one to the environment through movement in a place and through engagement with artifacts from the natural environment.

Song has the ability to speak to each intelligence and every learning style. Is it any wonder that song has the ability to cement itself in one's brain, even to the point that it can be irritating? Sometimes tunes get stuck in one's mind and they are not easily dispelled. Oliver Sacks (2007), a noted physician and professor of neurology, calls these catchy tunes "brainworms" (Sacks, 2007, p. 45). A "brainworm" could be quite handy at test time.

Learning songs engage learners. Songs make learning meaningful, exciting, and fun. They make learning easier for many students. Most people would find it easier to learn multiplication through song than by rote. Many would rather perform the song about Portland for family and friends than take a dry, written test about their town. Song, art, movement, dance, and presentation motivate students to want to learn.

Teaching through the creative modalities motivates students to want to come to school (Gullatt, 2007; Walker, 1995). When students are in school, engaged and involved, when they are receiving instruction in the learning language of their intelligence, academic achievement improves (Cade & Gunter, 2002; Ginns, 2005). Mnemonic song can provide students with the tools they need to succeed.

So how effective is mnemonic song for enhancing learning and memory, and how do musical mnemonics affect the diverse range of learning needs of elementary students? This question provokes an investigation as to how the phenomenon of mnemonic learning works. Neuroscientists and educators have been researching the effects of mnemonics for learning and memory retention, and they are using mnemonics as an intervention for diverse learners (Cade & Gunter, 2002; Paquette & Rieg, 2008; Scruggs & Mastropieri, 2000; Wolgemuth, Cobb, & Alwell, 2008).

The goal of our cognitively differentiated writing model is to maximize content learning used in the writing workshop. One modality that is particularly effective for enhancing learning and memory of content is song. Math and reading specialists alike have determined that a multisensory approach to learning is a more effective way to teach. We desire to adopt a similar pedagogy for writing. Since song is an especially effective teaching tool, we would like to further explore this learning modality.

New ideas may gain validity once we recognize and define what is wrong with the old ones. It is also easier to embrace change once we have perceived problems with past practices and perceptions. Part of the reason for our mindset about the arts is that modern educators have inherited a dissociated philosophy from ages past.

14

Inherited Dissociated Philosophy

The current system of education in the United States is built on a Western educational model, which divides learning into subjects and often views them as distinct and separate entities. Even at the elementary level, art, music, and physical education are considered their own subjects. Teachers have acquired the mindset that specialists must handle these disciplines.

The music or song that our study refers to is not professional instruction that requires specialists, but a utilitarian art form (song for the specific purpose of supporting an academic topic). On the other hand, it is not mindless silly singing that takes up time and adds little academic worth. While formal instruction in music does require a specialist, it does not take special skills to teach academics through song, movement, and art. It simply requires recognition of a need to accommodate different ways of knowing and learning.

A teacher must also have a desire to meet students' instructional needs in a more holistic way. One may not necessarily be musically inclined, artistically oriented, or be as physically fit as an Olympian; yet, it is still important to give all subjects a fair and equal presentation for students, regardless of personal strengths and weaknesses.

Unfortunately, due to the fact that educators have inherited a dissociated philosophy from ages past, they may have lost sight of the concept that all subjects of learning are intricately interconnected and deeply related. If one could draw that relationship, it would look like a thickly enmeshed Venn diagram, unlike the western model, which looks linear. When educators break subjects into their pieces and teach them in isolation, they can lose sight of how the subject is connected to the whole.

Many indigenous groups view all of life as interwoven and interrelated, like a thickly wound circle of rope (Kawagley, 2006).This philosophy helps educators understand why a linear, dissociated model is not an effective way to teach at the elementary level. First, if it feels disconnected and unrelated to teachers, it will feel disorganized and confusing to students. *Best practice* proposes that learning should be holistic and authentic. If all subjects are viewed as equally pertinent, potentially related, and integral to the whole body of knowledge, then it becomes apparent that they must be taught in the context of the whole. It also stands to reason that if a significant portion is omitted, then the whole body suffers (Gullatt, 2007).

Our study argues that a significant portion of the whole has been omitted from the curriculum. Some students are not receiving instruction in modalities that make comprehension possible for them; that dissociation and exclusion of a significant part of the whole has resulted in poor comprehension skills, inadequate memory ability, and low student achievement scores. These students struggle at test time because they cannot remember their lessons. It is likely they may not remember the lessons because they did not comprehend them in the first place. Perhaps students did not comprehend because the lessons were not delivered in the languages natural to their dispositions of knowing and learning.

If the use of the creative modalities for the purpose of academic instruction is not commonly seen today, it may be because education has lost sight of the whole. James Conner (1982), a developmental consultant, reports on research performed by Drs. Bernice McCarthy and Roger Sperry. McCarthy created a learning model partially based on the work of Nobel Laureate Dr. Sperry. In his Nobel lecture in 1982, Dr. Sperry's research demonstrated that brain functions may show left brain or right brain dominance, but the essence of his work gave rise to the understanding that all "normal people" are whole-brain thinkers. An editor for the journal *Leonardo,* Robert Root-Bernstein (2005), summarized Sperry's work:

> While he demonstrated that brain functions are lateralized, he also believed that consciousness arose from the interplay of the two hemispheres, or to use a term he coined, from being ambicerebral. This integrated view of the mind led him to reject both the Cartesian separation of mind and body, and C.P. Snow's division between sciences and humanities. (p. 224)

Sperry's research led him to believe that one needs to exercise and stimulate the whole brain, that science and art are interconnected and interrelated and should be viewed more holistically. Although Sperry earned a Nobel Prize for his work in medicine and physiology, he held a major in English literature, pursued the creative arts, and became an accomplished artist. Throughout his life, he was a man who strived to create bridges between science and art, and between theory and philosophy (Root-Bernstein, 2005).

After synthesizing the work of Sperry, Kolb, Piaget, and others, Dr. McCarthy created her 4MAT system for whole-brain learning, which she explains here:

> In my definition of learning, the learner makes meaning by moving through a natural cycle—a movement from feeling to reflecting to thinking, and finally, to acting. This cycle results from the interplay of two separate dimensions—perceiving and processing. (McCarthy, 1997, p. 49)

According to McCarthy, one perceives through feeling the experience, and then by thinking about it. One processes an experience by reflecting on it, and then by acting on that reflection. The places in the cycle where one feels most comfortable operating is what defines how one learns.

In order to determine what relationship exists between learning styles and right hemisphere-left hemisphere, and whole-brain processing preferences, McCarthy administered the Kolb Learning Style Inventory (Kolb, 1985) and the McCarthy Hemispheric Mode Indicator (McCarthy, 1986) to 2,367 teachers and administrators across all regions of the US and parts of Canada during 1986–1987 (McCarthy, 1987). From these surveys she further defined and classified four distinct learning tendencies. McCarthy diagramed the following four quadrants of learning, shown in table 14.1, and then arrived at this conclusion.

> Our whole educational system is based on the 'number two' learning style, on a reverence for the rational and analytical way of thinking, and on a low opinion of intuitive, creative ways, as well as on neglect of direct concrete experience. (Conner, 1982; McCarthy, 1987, 1997)

Their report says that schools are geared to teach to only 22% of the population. This leaves 78% shortchanged. They also feel that even the 22% for whom instruction is geared are short changed, in that they are being denied a whole range of cognitive and affective experiences (Conner, 1982).

Table 14.1. Four Learning Quadrants

Active/Experimentation (Doing)		Reflection/Observation (Watching)	
Dynamic learners (25%)	4	Innovative learners 1	(35%)
Common sense learners (18%)	3	Analytic learners 2	(22%)

After studying lateral specialization of cerebral function in epileptic patients who had had their brain hemispheres surgically separated, Dr. Sperry stated:

> The main theme to emerge from the following is that there appear to be two modes of thinking, verbal and nonverbal, represented rather separately in left and right hemispheres, respectively, and that our educational system, as well as science in general, tends to neglect the nonverbal form of intellect. What it comes down to is that modern society discriminates against the right hemisphere. (Sperry, 1973, p. 209)

Our study attempts to address cognitively differentiated strategies that will reach the needs of the remaining 78 percent of students who make up the typical classroom.

HISTORICAL BACKGROUND OF MNEMONIC LEARNING

For centuries, man has known that song provides a powerful mnemonic for learning. Yates (1956) recorded that ancient Greeks developed what he called the art of memory. The word *mnemonics* comes from their word called "mnemotechnics"—"mnemonikos" meaning "of memory" and "technics," which were techniques for using song, image, and place as a way to develop memory skills.

The Romans created memory theaters, imaginary rooms where an orator stored visual cues for parts of his speech. If his first topic was the price of corn, he would picture a husk of corn in a particular location to cue his memory. During the Middle Ages, singing bards, called jongleurs, would put important news to song in order to help them remember the key events that they reported to locals as they traveled from village to village.

Mao and Hitler both used song as their primary tool for indoctrinating children with propaganda. Ho and Law (2004) state, "Music and the other arts were required, according to Marxist-Leninist-Maoist ideology, to serve the interests of the workers, peasants, and soldiers to convey the messages of China's Communist government" (p. 153). Under Hitler and Mao, music in school was purely didactic, used strictly for teaching ideology and philosophy.

Most neuroscientists believe song is a biological mechanism, rather than a cultural invention, that music might be in our nature, like singing is for whales, dolphins, and birds (Peretz, 2006). Others see song as a social mechanism. Jensen (2000) stated, "Anthropologist Dr. Bruce Richman believes that singing lies part way between vocalizations (cries, sighs, and so on) and language (word, sentences, meaning, and so on). In fact, singing gives cultures something language cannot—social cohesion" (p. 22). Historically speaking, humans are musical. Music appears as naturally as language. For centuries man has enjoyed listening to music, creating music, and using music as a mnemonic aid, whether for nefarious or altruistic purposes.

Throughout the history of public education, value for music and the arts has gained and lost popularity. During the Dewey era (1910), music and the arts gained popularity with progressive educators and were thoroughly embraced by private schools serving affluent families. However, Professor Gullat (2007) reports, "The launch of the first Sputnik satellite in 1957 sent arts programs in schools back down to earth. Americans became consumed with mathematics and science education and saw the arts simply as frills" (pp. 215–216).

Unfortunately, some educators have adopted a mindset that music and the arts are not essential to core curriculum; that they are separate and dispensable subjects. Even though volumes of research studies demonstrate the academic value of the arts in the development of the whole child, when the budget axe falls, it is music and the arts that get placed on the chopping block.

15

Neuroscience of Music and Memory

As we've previously discussed, neuroscience has witnessed an explosion of information about the brain. New imaging techniques are allowing scientists to look into how the brain works and they are revolutionizing the understanding of the brain and unraveling some of its mysteries (Jefferies, Fritz, & Braun, 2003; Peretz, Gagnon, Herbert, & Macoir, 2004; Scruggs & Mastropieri, 2000).

One of these mysteries is how music affects the brain and memory. Neuromusical research is exploring how music affects the young mind, the old mind, brain-damaged patients, learning-disabled students, English language learners, and memory and learning in general. From recent research, neuromusical scientists postulate the basic following premises:

- The human brain has the ability to respond to and participate in music.
- The musical brain operates at birth and persists throughout life.
- Early and ongoing musical training affects the organization of the musical brain.
- The musical brain consists of extensive neural systems involving widely distributed, but locally specialized regions that include three components: cognitive, affective, and motor.
- The musical brain is highly resilient. (Hodges, 2000, p. 18)

Everyone, from cradle to the grave, can benefit from music.

There is evidence that formal training in music builds a better brain (Kilgour, Jakobson, & Cuddy, 2000). Diana Deutsch (2010), a professor of psychology who studies the perceptions of music and language, reports that musical training may even accelerate the process of learning to read. She cited a 2009 study that "found that eight-year-olds who had music lessons also showed better reading ability than the children who had instead learned to paint" (p. 3).

Jensen (2000) reports, "A Rockefeller foundation study found that music majors have the highest rate of admittance to medical school with a 66.7% acceptance rate" (p. 44). It is also documented that more musical training yields higher SAT scores (p. 45). Music has a powerful effect on the brain. Is it possible to harness some of this power for learning purposes?

MEMORY AND MUSIC

Researchers agree that there are different types of learning and memory systems. Sprenger (1998) defines five memory lanes and discusses how music connects to each one. She also describes each lane as a two-way street. One can store information through one lane, while receiving information through the opposing lane. She proposes that through music, one can teach in a way that will help students store information as well as retrieve that information. Sprenger (1998) asserted that song supports the five memory pathways in the following ways:

- **Semantic memory:** Song processes text and melody into one's long-term semantic memory through multiple repetitions over time.
- **Episodic memory:** Song activates episodic memory through a strong sense of place because music time generally happens in the same area, the song chart always rests in the same place, and movements are performed in the singing area as well.
- **Procedural memory:** Through song's natural kinesthetic processes, singing activates procedural memory. Adding actions and motions to a song create an even stronger physical connection to procedural memory.
- **Automatic memory:** Music is one of the most powerful ways to trigger automatic memory. Song lyrics and melodies activate a stimulus-response mechanism; both act as a cue for one another.
- **Emotional memory:** Because specific chemicals are released in the brain after emotional experiences, emotional memories are the most powerful memories and are often permanent. Singing, music, drama, role play, and artful experiences activate emotional memories (p. 67).

Sprenger concluded that an understanding of memory pathways gave her the tools to help students remember and learn in as many ways as possible.

Jensen (2000) records that music enhances the brain's memory system in two distinct ways. It activates attentional systems, because what we pay attention to we remember. "Music does this by increasing our attention to sounds and timing perception, while embedding emotional content" (p. 69). He also believed that music strengthens the five memory pathways. It aids memory because the beat, melody, and harmony serve as transmitters for the semantic content, which dramatically improves retention and recall. "This is why it is easier to recall the words to a song than a conversation" (p. 73).

MUSIC AND MNEMONICS

There is substantial evidence that mnemonic strategies enhance learning and memory (Cade & Gunter, 2002; Goll, 2004; Hodges, 1982; Jefferies, Fritz, Braun, 2003; Scruggs & Mastropieri, 2000; Wolgemuth, Cobb, & Alwell, 2008). Memories are stored in the hippocampus, which is part of the temporal lobe. The process of memory is called *encoding*. Short-term memories last less than half a second if they do not receive attention or recognition; they are simply forgotten. Attention-grabbing visual and aural devices, like mnemonic techniques, help keep information in the working memory. If the information is rehearsed, repeated, or practiced, then it can be transferred into long-term memory.

Dr. Goll (2004) states, "Psychologists identify two types of rehearsal—rote or repetition, which hold information in the memory for an immediate purpose and elaborative encoding which relates new information to that already in long-term memory" (p. 307).

Research documents that it is easier to learn and remember information using mnemonic methods because these techniques create an effective link of visual imagery and auditory cues to long-term memory. They also help bring organization to content that may not be inherently organized (Scruggs & Mastropieri, 2000). The most successful mnemonic devices are ones that create a structure for content, supply an easy to remember visual and aural representation of the information, and help facilitate future retrieval processes (Rainey & Larsen, 2002).

Song is a successful mnemonic device because it has the inherent characteristics just mentioned. By its nature, song is structured into verse and chorus with often repetitive phrases. The melodic and rhythmic elements, coupled with graphic representations for key words on the song chart, create musical patterns that are visually and aurally easy to remember. Song energizes emotional memory, while melody and text activate automatic memory, which makes song easy to recall (Crowder, Serafine, & Repp, 1990; Goll, 2004). When text is put to a familiar tune, recall is even greater (Rainey & Larsen, 2002).

Cognitive psychologists propose that long-term memory is organized in terms of schemata, or that which we know and have experienced. Vivid and sensual imagery techniques that are emotionally charged tie new information to old schema in a powerful way. For example, using the tune *O Christmas Tree,* one could teach the characteristics of an isosceles triangle with the following mnemonic:

> O Isosceles, O Isosceles, Two angles have equal degrees
> O Isosceles, O Isosceles, You look just like a Christmas tree
> You have three angles; You have three sides
> Two equal angles; Two equal sides
> O Isosceles, O Isosceles, You look just like a Christmas tree (Goll, 2004, p. 309)

Old schema instantly recognizes the shape of a Christmas tree. A Christmas song affects a strong emotional response. New schema powerfully connects to long-term memory so that it can become difficult to separate the two; long-term memory will associate an isosceles triangle with a Christmas tree. This phenomenon is what makes mnemonics a very successful device for learning-disabled students. It is effective because it relies on their strength of visual and acoustic memory rather than their weaknesses in semantic memory, prior knowledge, and the strength of independent recall (Scruggs & Mastropieri, 2000).

MNEMONICS AND DIVERSE LEARNERS

Since 1989, Scruggs and Mastropieri have been conducting research on the effect of mnemonic instruction with students who have special needs. One article describes a fourth grade teacher's application of mnemonic strategies to enhance student learning in her social studies class. Her class contained twenty-six children; five were classified as special education, twenty needed special supports, and only one showed the ability to work independently.

After examining her social studies curriculum, she began to think of mnemonic techniques to help teach concepts and vocabulary. For example, to help students remember that New World explorers came from Europe, she drew a sailboat with a rope and anchor dangling over the side. One of the stickmen in the boat had a speech bubble saying, "Pull up your rope, we're sailing to the New World" (Mastropieri, Sweda, & Scruggs, 2000, p. 71). Three times the teacher went over the keyword mnemonic that "your rope" equals Europe.

By comparing unit tests of material taught mnemonically to material that was not taught using mnemonics, her special education students demonstrated a 37.3% gain in content answered correctly using mnemonic aids. She concluded:

> Mnemonic strategy instruction for students with [learning disabilities] and other mild disabilities have been studied experimentally now for nearly 20 years, and it is clear from the evidence that it is extremely effective for meeting one critically important aspect of school learning—verbal memory for academic content. (Mastropieri et al., 2000, pp. 73–74)

An extensive amount of literature discusses the value of using songs for English language learners (Mora, 2000). Teachers of students of other languages find songs and chants valuable for cognitive, linguistic, and affective reasons. Stephen Krashen (1992), a well-known theorist of language acquisition, proposed the Affective Filter Hypothesis. He explains how the affective factors relate to language learning:

> If the acquirer is anxious, has low self-esteem, does not consider himself or herself to be a potential member of the group that speaks the language, he may understand the input, but it will not reach the language acquisition device—a block, the "Affective Filter," will keep it out. (Krashen, 1992, p. 6)

Wolfe (2006), a neuroeducator, further explains that when a person feels emotionally threatened, "The amygdala starts a chain of physiological responses (commonly called fight or flight response) to ready the body for action. Under these conditions, emotion is dominant over cognition, and the rational/thinking part of the brain is less efficient" (p. 4).

Teachers of English language learners recognize that in order for students to learn, they need to have a relaxed attitude and a positive, safe atmosphere. According to Schoepp (2001), "Songs are one method for creating an atmosphere that promotes language learning" (p. 2). Songs provide a method to learn English in a nonthreatening way. Because of their repetitive nature, songs create opportunities to practice words, phrases, and sentence patterns of conversational and colloquial English. Mnemonic songs have the ability to support a diverse range of learners through a modality that is fun.

ASSUMPTIONS AND FINAL THOUGHTS ON MNEMONIC SONG

Obviously, one cannot assume that all people are comfortable teaching through song. However, there are many children's learning songs on the market, so implementing song could be as easy as turning on a CD player. Yet some may still feel hesitant. An argument for incorporating song may be found in the elementary teacher's responsibility to give all subjects a reasonable amount of teaching time. Often teachers report that math is not their favorite subject or that technology is their weakness, yet all educators are expected to attain a certain measure of proficiency in these subjects and to teach them.

Conversely, our study on mnemonics does not intend to imply that teaching through mnemonic song is going to be a fix-all for what may be perceived as weaknesses in our educational system. Song is one technique that helps facilitate memory retention and recall of factual information. It cannot teach one how to think; it does not impart critical thinking skills, nor will it teach one how to infer meaning from text.

Song's strength lies in its ability to help cement the basic building blocks of learning into children's long-term memory. For instance, a test question may ask a student to make an inference regarding an isosceles triangle. Before a student can make an inference, he or she must first remember how to distinguish between an isosceles triangle, a right triangle, or a scalene triangle. Again, song may not help students to critically solve a mathematical word problem, but song can help facilitate verbatim recall of multiplication facts, which may be an essential skill in order to calculate the solution. Song can play a vital role in helping students be successful.

Song is a teaching tool that allows academics to be accessed by a greater number of learners and it is a technique that aids the memory. Song is just one type of mnemonic strategy, but it is one that contains a treasure trove of benefits. It makes learning meaningful and memorable for the child. It makes learning easier, and it makes learning fun.

16

Method and Practice
Putting It All Together

A child's school experience should be an amazing adventure, a joyous journey of discovery, and a special season where students are given opportunities to use their strengths, feel safe to expose their weaknesses, and are challenged to develop and grow. To ensure this is every child's school experience, educators may want to consider methods of instruction that address individual learning preferences and intelligences so that every student is offered an equal opportunity for success.

How does cognitively differentiated learning translate into classroom writing instruction? We believe this translates through a variety of cognitively differentiated teaching strategies, which means we try to integrate and horizontally differentiate curriculum as much as possible. We strive to create an intense synergy between academic subjects and the creative modalities so that we can reach as many learners as possible with content goals and objectives.

If we integrate language and content objectives and design lessons that specifically meet the needs of multiple intelligences and if we intentionally deliver instruction aurally, visually, kinesthetically, verbally, socially, and experientially, then we hope to level the learning field and make success available to all students. When we couple cognitively differentiated strategies with heavy modeling and lots of guided practice, we can make success irresistible.

Teachers' creative strengths vary considerably. Our talents happen to be song, movement, and art, yet there are no borders for the imagination. We have seen a middle school social science teacher use Dinah Zike's (1992) *Foldables* to turn history research and writing into an engaging, creative experience. We had a sixth grade teacher in San Francisco whose passion was photography. She built a dark room in one corner of our classroom and we studied marine life through field trips to the ocean and photography. There are myriad ways to design creative experiences for students. There is no right way or wrong way, just your way. Teachers should be encouraged to follow their passions and to teach through the modalities that they are excited about. Enthusiasm is contagious. Exposure to a variety of creative experiences enriches and expands children's educational journey.

As we create a writing lesson, we envision a wheel chart divided into the eight intelligences. The process of instruction moves around the wheel of intelligence using a prescribed method, where each day several intelligences have the opportunity to function within their strengths. Yet the daily goal is to teach through as many sensory modalities as possible so that we access and exercise as many intelligences as we can. We have created a diagram of a Cognitively Differentiated Writing Wheel to assist with lesson planning. (See figure 16.1.)

Using the Cognitively Differentiated Writing Wheel, we have outlined what one teaching–learning cycle looks like for a first through fifth grade

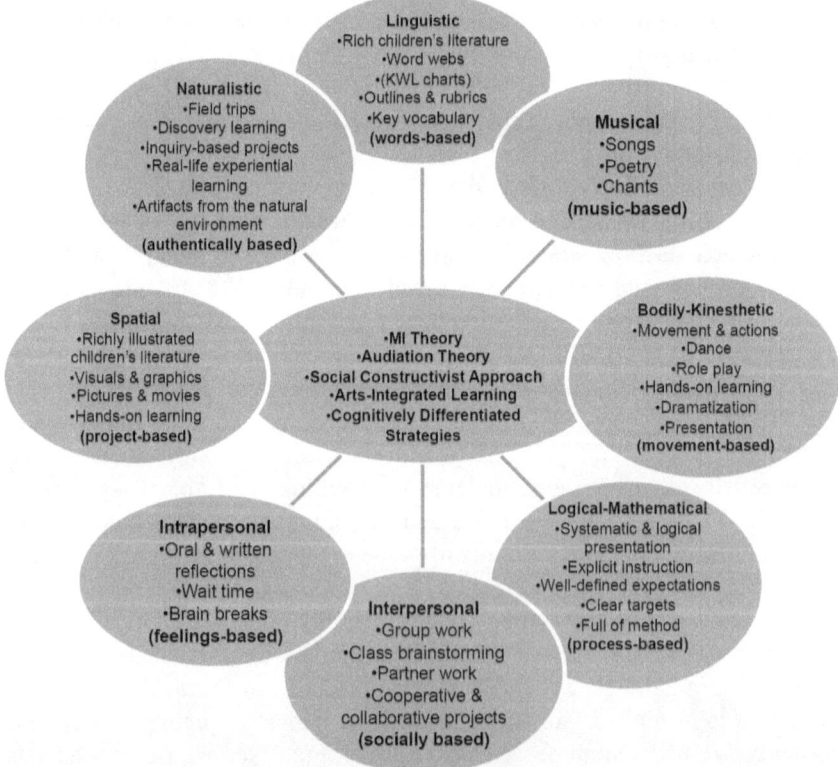

Figure 16.1. Cognitively Differentiated Writing Wheel

topic write. The following Sample Weekly Outline provides the structure and process for implementing our sentence-level writing intervention and cognitively differentiated writing model.

SAMPLE WEEKLY OUTLINE

Preliminary Preparation

1. **Immersion:** Saturate the classroom with meaningful and relevant content (Brechtel, 2001; Cambourne, 1998; Zemelman, Daniels, & Hyde, 2005).
2. **Teach to the Highest/Scaffold the Lowest:** Use literature, topic paragraphs for writing, song charts, and graphic organizers to support the highest reading level; scaffold the lowest through peer support and small-group instruction (Brechtel, 2000; Lemov, 2010).
3. **Add Graphics to Visuals:** Support English language learners by adding graphics to song charts, inquiry charts, graphic organizers, and word webs (Armstrong, 2000; Brechtel, 2005; Peregoy & Boyle, 2008; Sousa, 2007, 2011b).
4. **Post Writing Outlines, Models, and Rubrics:** Place writing outlines and rubrics in a visually accessible place in the classroom (Armstrong, 2000; Cambourne, 1998; Pudewa, 2015; Sousa, 2007, 2011b; Webster, 1994).
5. **Activate Prior Knowledge:** Have students create a KWL (what I *know*, what I *want* to know, and what I have *learned*) chart on the topic (Harvey & Goudvis, 2007; Keene & Zimmermann, 2007).

Monday: (Linguistic, Musical, Kinesthetic, Logical-Mathematical)

1. Scaffold learning through a "read aloud" about the topic (Krashen, 2003; Sousa, 2007, 2011a; Vygotsky, 1934).
2. Scaffold learning of main topic and key vocabulary through a song, adding actions whenever it's practical (Armstrong, 2000; Gardner, 1999).
3. Have students perform a shared read of a summary paragraph about the topic that the teacher has prepared from the "read aloud" (Fountas & Pinnell, 2001).
4. Ask students to create a Key Word Outline of the contentives from the topic paragraph and record on a three- by five-inch index card (Keene & Zimmerman, 2007; Pudewa, 2015; Webster, 1994).
5. Allow students to retell the topic's main points from their Key Word Outline (Harvey & Goudvis, 2007; Keene & Zimmerman, 2007; Pudewa, 2015).

Tuesday: (Logical-Mathematical, Musical, Kinesthetic, Spatial, Linguistic)

1. Sing learning song with actions.
2. Use the Key Word Outline and Writing Matrix, ask students to brainstorm essential Dress-Ups into the Writing Matrix using quality adjectives, strong verbs, "ly" words, who/which clauses, prepositional phrases, because clause, and adverb clauses (when, while, where, as, since, if, although, because).
3. As a class, have students use the Key Word Outline, Writing Matrix, and the writing rubrics to write their rough drafts. Students underline their Dress-Ups. (In the beginning the teacher assists, models, and demonstrates what great writing looks like. When students understand the process, they begin working with a partner, and then gradually work toward independence) (Peregoy & Boyle, 2008; Pudewa, 2015).
4. Ask students to open their sentences six different ways (ten for older students). They number and circle them in the left margin as they write (Pudewa, 2015; Webster, 1994).

Wednesday: (Interpersonal, Musical, Kinesthetic, Linguistic)

1. Sing learning song with actions.
2. Ask students to peer edit and then edit with teacher. Students write their final drafts on thematic stationary (see figures 16.5 and 16.7). Have students read their composition to a friend and then have a few students read theirs to the class.

Thursday: (Intrapersonal, Musical, Kinesthetic, Linguistic, Interpersonal)

1. Sing learning song with actions.
2. Ask students to write a brief reflection on the "Most Interesting Fact" for what they have learned about the topic. They should do this with no assistance from the teacher.
3. Encourage students to write without assistance in their My Journal on any topic of their choice. For those reticent writers, teacher may offer a prompt or creative story starter. Their My Journal and "Most Interesting Fact" become an accurate record of their personal growth as a writer. It provides an authentic assessment tool for teaching and learning, especially when the teacher provides immediate feedback (Cambourne, 1998).
4. Have students share their journal write with a partner and with the class (Fountas & Pinnel, 2001).

Friday: (Spatial, Naturalistic, Kinesthetic)

Method and Practice: Putting It All Together 107

1. Instruct students to create an art project that supports the topic and assemble their thematic journals. Students create a thematic journal on a twelve-by-eighteen-inch piece of construction paper folded to create four pages (see figures 16.2 and 16.8). Its pages consecutively house the title, name, and Most Interesting Fact (figures 16.3 and 16.6); artwork (figures 16.5 and 16.7); writing (figures 16.5 and 16.7); and song (figures 16.4 and 16.8). These journals are hung on display in the hall or classroom for parents and students to enjoy. Their thematic journals form a large part of their semester portfolio and serve as a significant assessment piece (Armstrong, 2000; Cambourne, 1998; Gardner, 1999; Jensen, 2000, 2005).

Winter and Spring Presentations: (All intelligences)

Toward the end of each semester, students share their learning through speech, song, movement, and drama for their parents and friends. This is a culminating event, as well as a celebration of learning (Cambourne, 1998; Jensen, 2000; Gardner, 1999; Pudewa, 2015).

In summary, the teaching–learning cycle for this writing model should include:

1. Explicit skills-based instruction of the specific elements found in effective sentences
2. Guided practice, teacher and peer modeling, shared writes, partner work, and peer editing
3. Independent work and final drafts
4. Arts-integrated content learning activities
5. Regular celebrations of learning

Figure 16.2.

Figure 16.3.

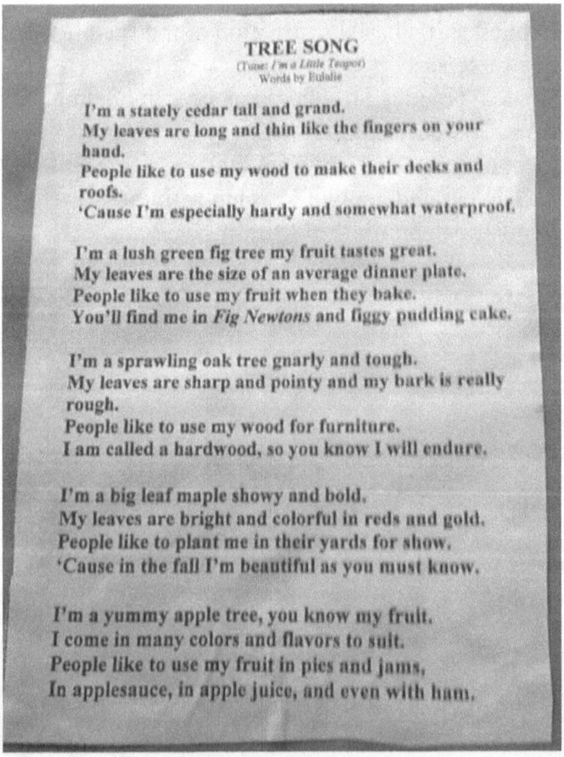

Portland's Trees

Most Interesting Fact

Figure 16.4.

TREE SONG
(Tune: *I'm a Little Teapot*)
Words by Eulalie

I'm a stately cedar tall and grand.
My leaves are long and thin like the fingers on your hand.
People like to use my wood to make their decks and roofs.
'Cause I'm especially hardy and somewhat waterproof.

I'm a lush green fig tree my fruit tastes great.
My leaves are the size of an average dinner plate.
People like to use my fruit when they bake.
You'll find me in *Fig Newtons* and figgy pudding cake.

I'm a sprawling oak tree gnarly and tough.
My leaves are sharp and pointy and my bark is really rough.
People like to use my wood for furniture.
I am called a hardwood, so you know I will endure.

I'm a big leaf maple showy and bold.
My leaves are bright and colorful in reds and gold.
People like to plant me in their yards for show.
'Cause in the fall I'm beautiful as you must know.

I'm a yummy apple tree, you know my fruit.
I come in many colors and flavors to suit.
People like to use my fruit in pies and jams,
In applesauce, in apple juice, and even with ham.

Figure 16.5.

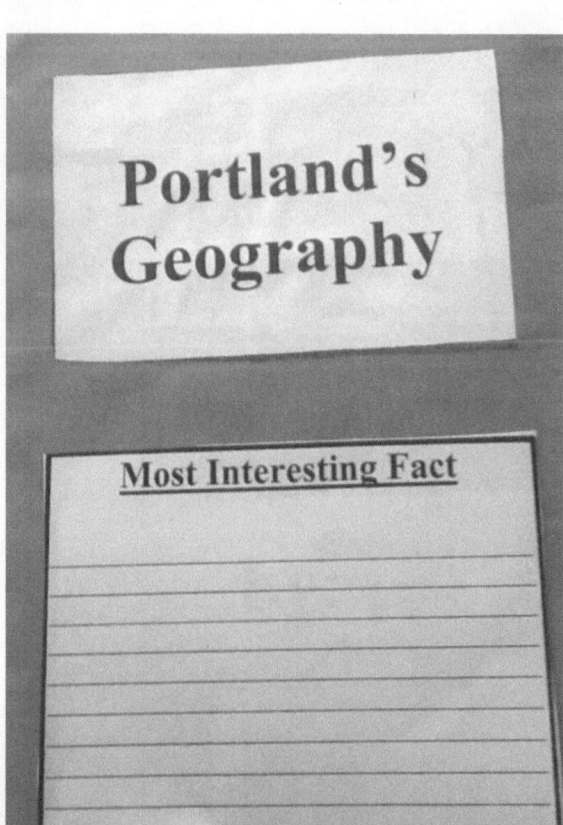

Figure 16.6.

Figure 16.7.

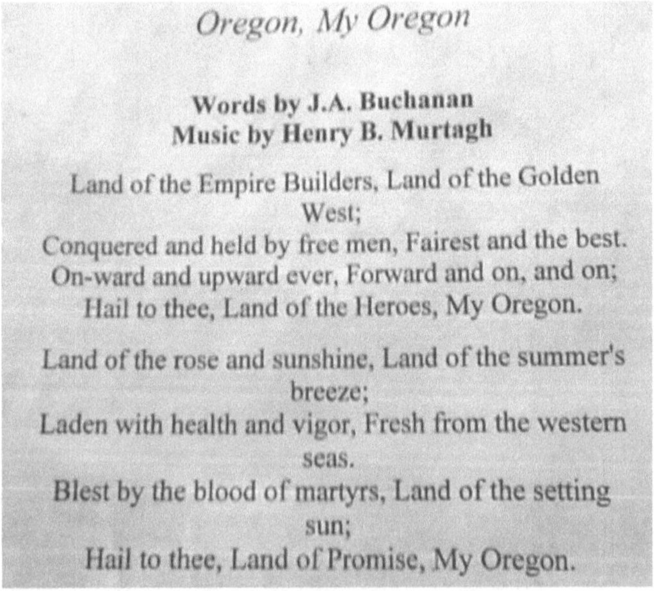

Oregon, My Oregon

Words by J.A. Buchanan
Music by Henry B. Murtagh

Land of the Empire Builders, Land of the Golden West;
Conquered and held by free men, Fairest and the best.
On-ward and upward ever, Forward and on, and on;
Hail to thee, Land of the Heroes, My Oregon.

Land of the rose and sunshine, Land of the summer's breeze;
Laden with health and vigor, Fresh from the western seas.
Blest by the blood of martyrs, Land of the setting sun;
Hail to thee, Land of Promise, My Oregon.

Figure 16.8.

17

Best Practice for Writing Instruction

The new millennium requires an explicit, multimodal, cognitively differentiated approach to writing instruction—a method that begins with the rudiments of sentence construction and teaches writing with learning aptitudes in mind. Starting from a social constructivist approach, which is the basis of creative arts pedagogy, learning is explicit and systematic, and then it is modeled and practiced through a variety of modalities that differentiate for different dispositions of knowing and learning. Horizontal differentiation provides students fairer and more equal access to content; therefore, it provides an equal opportunity for success.

Most learners want to know and see the plan for what is required of them; they want clear, well-defined expectations and goals. Most of us resent being held hostage to an abstract or vague expectation hidden within the instructor's mind. It is unfair to expect students to play the game "Guess My Expectation!" Yet when it comes to writing instruction, this has seemingly been an acceptable strategy for a century or more.

It is time to restructure our method for elementary writing instruction. Educators should consider a more explicit and progressive approach, starting with the basic building blocks of sentence construction. We should systematically teach the structure, craft, and techniques of sentence writing and post clearly defined outlines and rubrics of the forms and varieties of elements that are found in great compositions. Students should practice the structure and style of writing using social constructivist strategies.

Using "read alouds" and oral-based guided practice, we should scaffold students' learning and help them build a lexicon of phrasing patterns so that eventually they may be able to audiate complex language patterns on their own. To accommodate the neurodiversity of young learners, educators in the new millennium should also recognize that we must teach to the variety of ways that students learn. This integrated, cognitively differentiated model endeavors to apply the latest research from neuroscience and best practice (Zemelman, Daniels, & Hyde, 2005) to create an elementary writing model that is skills-based, yet accommodates for the neurodiversity of learners.

It is an odd thing, but it seems that research and best practice strongly support multimodal, experiential, right-brain learning, yet the pendulum of practice seems to be consistently moving more strongly toward left-brain–oriented teaching strategies. Daniel Pink (2006), in his book *A Whole New Mind: Why Right-Brainers Will Rule the Future,* claims that during the Information Age of the twentieth century, L-Directed (logical, analytical) Thinking, the characteristics and aptitudes of left hemisphere thinkers, was highly prized and valued. The dominant fields of science and technology demanded sequential, literal, functional, logical, and analytic thinkers.

Its counterpart, R-Directed (creative, intuitive) Thinking, on the other hand, has often been disdained and dismissed as inessential. Pink (2006) believes value for hemispheric preference is about to change. He claims that we are about to enter a new age: the Conceptual Age. This era will usher in a greater appreciation for artistry, synthesis, ingenuity, intuition, emotional expression, and holistic thinking. Pink (2006) asserts:

> Today, the defining skills of the previous era—the "left-brain" capabilities that powered the Information Age—are necessary but no longer sufficient. And the capabilities we once disdained or thought frivolous—the "right-brain" qualities of inventiveness, empathy, joyfulness, and meaning—increasingly will determine who flourishes and who flounders. (p. 3)

Because of forces beyond teachers' control—Common Core State Standards and the worst recession since the Great Depression—the emphasis of education has become standards-based assessments that document AYP. Coupled with funding cuts, which has often resulted in the elimination of most art, music, and physical education programs, schools are being propelled on a left-brain trajectory.

As schools succumb to the pressure of performing well on AYP assessments, and as funding for education continues to decline, schools seem to be resurrecting the factory model of the Industrial Age. With the ever-increasing demands for teacher and school accountability, it has become all about the bottom line—producing a desired set of test scores. It feels as if we are striving to create a production line of children who can score well on tests.

Children are not automatons. Neither are their brains. Some of today's school practices remind us somewhat of the old-time practices of some western horsemen. They approached a horse with the idea that they should dominate it and force it to submit. When they set out to "break" a horse, they literally set out to conquer and subdue its will. For this type of horseman, the objective was 100 percent about what he needed from the horse; there was not much concern for what was good for the animal.

The educated horseperson approaches a horse from an entirely different perspective. He or she believes one begins by "gentling" the horse, by first trying to win its trust. The horseperson tries to establish a relationship with the animal by learning to speak "equus." He or she attempts to communicate with the animal using behavioral language that the horse understands.

Training begins by allowing the horse to run free in a round pen. The horseperson gently asks the horse to trot around the pen, urging the horse on with either a coiled rope or a long lunging whip. Without looking the horse in the eye, which communicates predatorial behavior to a prey animal, the horseperson politely asks the horse to submit to his or her leadership and allow him or her to become the alpha horse. When the horse is ready, the horse drops its nose toward the ground, and as the horse trots, it starts to lick and chomp its lips. This behavior lets the horseperson know that the horse has given his or her permission to become alpha in the human–horse relationship. At this point the horseperson drops the arm holding the rope, turns a shoulder to the animal, and stands still. When the horse walks up to the horseperson, and allows the person to pet it, then the horse has chosen the person, and the alpha-bond is formed.

For the educated horseperson, the objective is 100 percent about establishing a relationship with the horse; it is about learning to speak the horse's language and it is about approaching the animal on the animal's terms. The modern horseperson who has studied horse behavior knows that we may communicate with the animal through body language that mimics similar actions seen in herd behavior. By speaking to the horse in a language it understands, the horse learns that it may trust the human. After a bond of trust has been formed, the horse is generally willing to do whatever work it is asked to do. By using a symbol-processing system that the horse understands, the horseperson is able to foster a relationship that is sensitive and caring toward the animal.

Would the typical child in today's classrooms say that his or her school's main objective is a concern for individual learning needs? Would the child feel instruction is given in a language that is natural to his or her ability to learn? Could the child say that someone cares about his or her learning language? Would most children say that school is relevant, meaningful, and rewarding? Is our educational system sensitive and caring toward children's physical, emotional, social, and intellectual needs? Are we inviting a teaching and learning relationship that accommodates the different ways that students learn? Or are today's educational objectives mostly about what adults want and need? Would most elementary teachers say that they have the liberty to apply best practices (Zemelman et al., 2005) in their classrooms, or would they say that various demands from their district and state supersede their students' learning needs?

We believe all of these questions should be addressed. We believe that a cognitively differentiated writing model may provide a practical solution for some of these concerns. Not only will it help educators to meet the academic goals required by their state, but also, the multimodal strategies differentiate academic content to accommodate for the neurodiversity of young learners.

Through the writing workshop, teachers may apply best practices, may teach the foundations of writing skills acquisition, and may rehearse and review grade-level content goals required to demonstrate AYP, yet do so through methods that are sensitive and considerate of how students learn.

Excellence in best practice is more than encouraging students to score well on their assessments. Most educators have observed that a few students seem to excel in school, whereas others struggle to succeed. A few seem to be born with the gifts and talents that foster scholarship and make school easy, yet most appear to lack those advantages, making school difficult. In reality, each student has an area where he or she excels and it is an effective educator who discovers that area in a child. The thoughtful teacher in the new millennium understands that best practice brings excellence out of the students who cannot find it in themselves.

18

Training Teachers for the New Millennium

We both attest that in our respective teaching colleges we were offered explicit instruction on how to teach reading and math, but very little on how to teach writing. We were taught how to teach music and art, but again, very little on how to use these modalities to support academic content learning. Teaching programs should offer classes on how to teach the rudiments of writing at the sentence level. Novice teachers should leave their educational institutions feeling equipped to teach sentence structure and style.

With the idea of using the arts as a pedagogical teaching tool comes the idea that education programs ought to be training student teachers how to use the arts in their teaching practice. Teaching colleges could offer training in the use of this sentence-level writing intervention and this cognitively differentiated writing model to provide those entering the teaching profession the confidence and skill to teach writing and to incorporate arts-integrated strategies as part of an educator's pedagogical repertoire.

Amazingly enough, Australia and China are already embracing a transformational move towards arts-integrated education. Emerging out of their examination-driven cultures is an overhaul of existing curricula that encourages the development of intellectual inquiry, critical thinking, and creativity that is both sensitive to the arts and provides novice educators confidence to teach through a variety of modalities. Mark Selkrig and Christine Bottrell (2009), from La Trobe University in Victoria, Australia, report on a unique education program for student teachers that require aspiring educators to study both visual and performing arts as an instructional discipline:

> Education "in" and "through" the arts has been identified as a powerful vehicle in assisting students to understand their world and providing students with a

range of positive influences on approaches and attitudes of learning. Growing evidence indicates that educators should seriously consider the role the arts can play in their pedagogical practice, regardless of the age of the student or the learning discipline that they teach. (p. 395)

Rather than just theorizing about constructivist ideas of teaching and learning, Selkrig and Bottrell (2009) suggest that teachers ought to provide students opportunities to participate in a gamut of constructive experiences that incorporate a variety of symbol-processing systems. Hence, by exposing student teachers to a range of art-making techniques, such as drawing, printmaking, painting, sculpting, multimedia, drama, dance, and music, Australia hopes to develop teacher confidence and skill to use these multiple modalities of learning (p. 401).

David Campion (2011), a Fulbright Scholar in Hong Kong and junior associate professor at Lewis and Clark College in Portland, Oregon, reports that Hong Kong's higher education is embracing the liberal arts. This new curriculum is being instituted largely in response to demand from local employers. Companies in Hong Kong have been complaining that universities are turning out graduates who are well-trained and competent in their specialties, but they lack broad vision, imagination, and the critical thinking skills necessary for advanced leadership positions (p. B7).

Hong Kong intends to overhaul existing curricula to parallel the liberal arts model pioneered by American colleges and universities, adding an additional year to all their bachelor's degree programs to include a wide range of coursework in the humanities, social and natural sciences, and the creative arts. Campion (2011) cautions:

> It should cause considerable unease in the United States, since our system of higher education appears increasingly to be moving in the opposite direction. Many of our public universities across the country, facing unprecedented budget reductions, are enacting draconian cuts in established programs. In a few cases, they are eliminating them altogether. Indeed, the arts and humanities have been particularly hard hit, since these tend to be perceived by some administrators as having limited value in generating income for their institutions. Likewise, they are viewed all too often as frivolous use of valuable tuition dollars and poor preparation for a highly competitive job market. (p. B7)

Campion (2011) concludes by pointing out that the lesson we could learn from Hong Kong is that "the most vibrant and diversified economies will continue to demand the very qualities in higher education that have long been the strengths of our universities, but which we are currently devaluing" (p. B7).

Mariale Hardiman (2003), interim dean of the Johns Hopkins University School of Education and author of *Connecting Brain Research with Effective Teaching: The Brain-Targeted Teaching Model*, writes:

> The strength of a nation, the very backbone of success in a global economy, depends on a workforce capable of creativity and innovation. Yet, as leaders lament, many students leave school lacking those essential skills. Educating citizens of tomorrow will require the redesign of school policies and practices so that students are not merely acquiring information, but also are applying knowledge in novel ways. (pp. 227–228)

Many educators who work at the elementary level have grave concerns for our children's future success. Some of our students are growing up in an educational system that has been stripped of every opportunity for creative and innovative development. During these economically depressed times, not only have art, music, physical education, and recess been either cut or severely reduced, but the creative, active, fun part of the school day has been replaced by ninety-minute, back-to-back workshops, often accompanied with heavily scripted curricula that allows precious little time or liberty to implement a more arts-integrated approach to learning. The focus has become so examination driven that we have inadvertently excised most of the motivational reasons children love school.

During our childhood, if you had asked us why we loved school, we would have responded, "Because we loved recess, physical education, music, and art." Learning was a byproduct, but our motivation to learn was maintained and stimulated via the elements of education that made learning fun. Some teachers are worried for their students because their schools have become so underfunded and so examination driven that they have been stripped of the creative elements that make learning rewarding for students.

Melissa McNeil (2011), a fourth/fifth grade teacher at Central Point Elementary in Oregon, reports that in her eight years of teaching, she has never known a school year that was not made difficult by budget cuts. She reiterates a similar sentiment in *Today's OEA:*

> I'm frustrated with the state for not funding us, and for the national government for setting unrealistic expectations that will set us up for failure. McNeal said, "One hundred percent passing a test? Really?" And how is the test even remotely useful as an indicator of student progress? It is a post mortem, plain and simple. I could be more supportive of testing if it either was based on growth of the student, or was in any way, shape or form remotely useful as a tool for my teaching. But I don't believe it helps me meet the needs of any of my kids. I can't bear to think that these kids are getting an elementary experience devoid

of everything that I loved when I was a kid. But testing is always there. The kids know it. I know it. We can't escape it. (p. 21)

All work and no play make learning an unbearable experience for most children. From a child's perspective, learning needs to be engaging, meaningful, and fun, or their interest quickly wanes. Yes, we can coerce students to stay in their seats with either the threat of negative consequences or through a constant barrage of positive incentives, but again we should ask, "Is this 'cram-for-the-test' approach to learning sensitive to the needs of most children?"

Referring to the analogy of the old-time western horseman, in hindsight the modern, educated horseperson looks back on the training practices used in the past and is horrified at the barbaric methods. We wonder, are educators going to look back on this era of high-stakes testing and view those practices with a similar remorse?

Maybe our profession should adopt its own version of the Hippocratic Oath to outline a pedagogical framework that should be adhered to as the pendulum of practice swings from one extreme to the other. Perhaps the following adaptation would help us not to lose sight of the big picture for our practice.

HIPPOCRATIC OATH FOR EDUCATORS

1. I swear to fulfill, to the best of my ability and judgment, this covenant.
2. I will respect the hard-won scientific gains of those educators in whose steps I walk, and gladly share such knowledge as is mine with those who are to follow.
3. I will create a physical learning environment that promotes a positive emotional climate and design learning experiences that are sensitive to the physical, emotional, and intellectual needs of the whole child—and understand that sometimes warmth, sympathy, and understanding may outweigh administrative goals and objectives.
4. I will apply, for the benefit of all my students, a variety of multisensory teaching techniques and strategies so that each student may receive academic content via the symbol-processing systems that are natural to his or her ability to learn.
5. I will remember that teaching is an art as well as a science, that several intelligences are arts based, and that there is a multisensory magic to teaching and learning when I use the arts as a teaching methodology throughout curricula.
6. I will not be ashamed to say, "I need help," nor will I fail to call on my colleagues when the skills of another are needed for my students to learn.

7. I will respect and nurture an understanding for all cultures, races, and religions, and will strive to focus on the commonalities and values that bind us together and foster unity among the human race.
8. I will remember that I do not educate a test score or statistical measure, but a sensitive human being, whose learning needs may be affected by the person's family situation or economic circumstance. My responsibility includes understanding and compassion for these related issues if I am to teach and adequately care for the whole child.
9. I will promote learning in whatever way I can, realizing that the neural, physical, emotional, and cultural diversity of learners demands differentiation.
10. I will remember that I remain a member of my community and my society, with special obligation to all my fellow human beings, those sound of body and mind as well as those with special needs.
11. If I do not violate this oath, may I enjoy life and art, respected while I live and remembered with affection thereafter. May I always act so as to preserve the finest traditions of my calling and may I long experience the joy of teaching those placed in my care. (Adapted from Louis Lasagna, 1964.)

Teaching colleges are always in pursuit of excellence. *Best Practice* (Zemelman, Daniels, & Hyde, 2005) has ingrained in all of us that the best teaching strategies are experiential, holistic, expressive, and interactive—that dynamic learning is relevant, meaningful, and fun. We believe educators will see the worth of offering students explicit outlines and clearly defined rubrics as they learn to write. We know that a cognitively differentiated approach to teaching defines the essence of best practice.

It is our hope that this book will be used as standard curricula in teaching colleges across America, so that all aspiring educators leave their training programs feeling confident they can teach writing at the sentence level using cognitively differentiated strategies. In Appendix D, we have included a Sample Syllabus for a semester class. By providing a visual of course goals and objectives, we hope college administrators will see that this instruction fills an area of need in teacher's preparatory coursework. We need their help if we are to effect change and pursue excellence in writing instruction.

19

Final Reflection

"Diversity is the order of the new millennium," declares Gardner (1999, p. 217). If the past millennium has ushered in greater democracy, this one should usher in greater appreciation for diversity. Recognizing and respecting each person's unique genetic blueprint sparks myriad ways for the individual to make a unique contribution to the world. The Earth is now a global village. This millennium demands a more holistic, integrated world view.

Everyone recognizes the importance of science and technology because they have defined for people general principles and universal laws; yet it is the arts and humanities that exalt the uniqueness of individual spirit and document the craft, creativity, and ingenuity of humans. The task for the new millennium is to hone the creative and innovative skills that inspire imagination, critical reasoning, and new ways of thinking.

This means educators must embrace and use differentiated techniques that accommodate cognitive diversity and integrate a multidisciplinary, multiintelligence, multimodal approach for learning so that an educational system can be constructed that offers all students an equal opportunity for development and success. Working together, parents and educators could morally, culturally, and academically create more holistic schools, which in turn would build a better, more beautiful world and, according to Gardner (1999), "a world in which a great variety of people will want to live" (p. 4).

The emphasis of this writing intervention has been threefold: to explicitly teach the structure and style of sentence construction, to provide neurologically sound reasons explaining why academic content should be delivered via the natural symbol-processing systems of learners, and to visually construct a model for what a sentence-level writing intervention and cognitively differentiated writing approach looks like. Models provide a structure for organizing materials and thoughts. This structural model gives precise instructions as to the specific sentential elements that should be found within elementary compositions and provides multimodal techniques for delivering academic writing content in the multiple languages of learners.

Constructing a composition is somewhat analogous to building a house. If one imagines that paragraphs are the rooms, and sentences represent the way we decorate the rooms, then one could picture how each room has its own distinct structure and style. Each room has its own unique function and each room is decorated accordingly.

Much like we dress up a room with paint, carpets, furniture, wallpaper, drapes, and pictures, in like manner we dress up our sentences with quality adjectives, strong verbs, "ly" words, adjective clauses, adverb clauses, and prepositional phrases. Just as each room opens before us and delights the eye with a variety of colors and décor, so too, our sentences should intrigue the eye with a variety of sentence openers. Like a room, a paragraph should neither be bare nor boring. A variety of Dress-Ups, Sentence Openers, and Decorations are the tools we need to construct interesting and engaging compositions (Webster, 1994).

One can also appreciate that the occupants of each room will desire different décors. Dad's den will look very different from Mom's kitchen or daughter's bedroom. Just as we decorate different rooms according to each individual's personal tastes and preferences, in the same way we teach academic writing content though a variety of modalities to accommodate for preferences of learning styles and intelligences. Just as each room reflects the personality and style of its occupants, so too, knowledge illuminates individual understanding through a variety of symbol-processing systems that represent the different languages of learners.

If we teach students to construct compositions using well-defined sentential structure and style, and teach the content for writing through differentiated multimodal techniques, then students will learn the art of designing effective, sophisticated sentences, as well as enhance their retention of academic content through a variety of memory-enhancing techniques, which are naturally embedded in this cognitively differentiated writing workshop.

This model provides the specifics and parameters necessary to build syntactically interesting sentences. When the sentence-level writing intervention is used in conjunction with an existing writing program, students will receive comprehensive instruction in the forms, phrases, clauses, functions, process, and principles of writing assessment. Because most current writing curricula thoroughly teach functions, process, and principles of assessment, our goal was to complement and complete these works, not to duplicate what has already been done well. Hence, we limited our language objectives strictly to teaching the building blocks of sentence construction, but we also emphasized content objectives through a novel approach that uses multimodal teaching strategies.

In conclusion, weaving sentence-level writing with multisensory instruction creates a tapestry of complex cognitive processes. These processes support a cognitively differentiated elementary writing model that is neurally, physically, emotionally, and culturally responsive, breaking down the forces of marginalization commonly experienced in traditional classrooms. This intervention facilitates the mechanics of crafting sentences while using the arts as a teaching methodology throughout curricula in an effort to accomplish the following:

- To aggregate all components of the writing process
- To accommodate for the neurodiversity of all learners
- To advocate for balanced pedagogical practices that make academics accessible to all learners

We believe this writing intervention demystifies the elusive sentence; it is a primer for writing skills acquisition that plainly and precisely defines the rudiments of writing. We also hold that this cognitively differentiated writing model produces a kind of student success that sings with diversity, dances with creativity, and plays with the orchestration of written composition. It teaches young writers the music of words so they may create their own sentential symphonies, striving to provide even the most hesitant composers—a song of hope.

Appendix A
Arts-Integrated Resources

ARTS-BASED LEARNING

Carratello, P. (2004). *My body.* Westminster, CA: Teacher Created Resources.
Foster, W. (2005). *Draw and color sea creatures.* Laguna Hills, CA: Walter Foster.
———. (2006a). *Draw and color insects.* Laguna Hills, CA: Walter Foster.
———. (2006b). *Draw and color reptiles & amphibians.* Laguna Hills, CA: Walter Foster.
Harpster, S. (2010). *Drawing animals with numbers.* Ashland, OH: Harptoons.
———. (2010). *Pencil, paper, draw: Animals.* Ashland, OH: Harptoons.
———. (2010). *Pencil, paper, draw: Cars & trucks.* Ashland, OH: Harptoons.
———. (2010). *Pencil, paper, draw: Dinosaurs.* Ashland, OH: Harptoons.
———. (2010). *Pencil, paper, draw: Dogs.* Ashland, OH: Harptoons.
———. (2010). *Pencil, paper, draw: Flowers.* Ashland, OH: Harptoons.
———. (2010). *Pencil, paper, draw: Horses.* Ashland, OH: Harptoons.
———. (2010). *Pencil, paper, draw: Sharks.* Ashland, OH: Harptoons.
Milliken, L. (2007). *American patriotic symbols activity book.* Fort Atkinson, WI: Highsmith.
Mangrum, K. (2008). *How to draw: Step-by-step using the alphabet.* Bloomington, IN: Author House.
Morton, P. (1991). *Educator's activity book about bats.* Austin, TX: Bat Conservation International.
Pallotta, J. (2003). *How to draw icky bugs.* New York, NY: Scholastic.

Appendix A

SONG-BASED LEARNING

Beall, P. C., & Nipp, S. H. (1987). *Wee sing America.* New York, NY: Price Stern Sloan.

Eldon, D., & Eldon, D. (2003). *Lyrical life science* (vol. 1, 2, & 3). Corvallis, OR: Lyrical Learning.

Some key topics the Eldons teach through song:

- The scientific method
- Invertebrates
- Coldblooded vertebrates
- Birds
- Plants
- Bats
- Whales
- The skeletal system
- The muscular system
- The nervous system

Gentner N. (1997). *B-B-B-Bats.* Chicago IL: McGraw Hill.
Gentner N. (1993). *Bear Facts.* Chicago IL: McGraw Hill.
Gentner N. (1995). *Frog on a log.* Chicago IL: McGraw Hill.
Gentner N. (1993). *Munch, munch, munch!* Chicago IL: McGraw Hill.
Gentner N. (1995). *Save a tree for me.* Chicago IL: McGraw Hill.
Meish, G. (2006). *Mnemonic songs for content area learning.* New York, NY: Scholastic.

Some key topics Meish teaches through song:

- Eight parts of speech
- Adjectives that compare
- Parts of a story
- Similes and metaphors
- Personification
- The writing process
- Provide details
- Avoid tired words
- Rivers and mountains
- The pilgrims
- The thirteen colonies
- The Oregon trail
- U.S. presidents
- Civil rights
- Women's rights
- -Ology
- Scientific classifications
- How the heart works

- Parts of the brain
- Water cycle
- Parts of plants

Troxel, K. (1994). *Grammar songs.* Newport Beach, CA: Audio Memory.
Walz, P., & McLaughlin, P. (2009). *Memory-boosting mnemonic songs: Grammar.* New York, NY: Scholastic.

Websites

http://discoverandlearn.net
www.songsforteaching.com

SONG-BASED LEARNING BY EULALIE

Through the years, Leta and Eulalie have needed learning songs for specific content topics for math and writing workshops. While we initially tried to search for existing songs, when we were designing multimodal units there were not many resources on the market. Troxel's *Grammar Songs* and the Eldons' *Lyrical Life Sciences* have been around since the 1980s and 1990s, respectively, although Goldish's *Mnemomic Songs* have only been available since 2006. Consequently, when we could not find what we needed, Eulalie created her own repertoire of learning songs. Many times teachers have asked her to share her materials.

Eulalie will soon be publishing her learning songs for writing, social science, and science to complement the works we have listed. Added to that list are two multimodal units called *Math, Music, & Motion* and *World Geography, Music, & Mapping.* Because we teach math and geography through the story of song, the lyrics may be used to practice adverb clauses (*when, while, where, as, since, if, although, because*). This provides an excellent opportunity to integrate some writing practice within our math workshop or geography lesson. For instance, the teacher could have students brainstorm sentences (such as the following) from whatever song they are learning.

> **When** I skip count by three five times, it will equal fifteen.
> **While** herding ducks in groups of four, fox learned to multiply by four.
> **Where** three 12-inch rulers sit end-to-end, one could fit one yard stick.
> **As** you near the Arctic Circle, you will see the northern lights and fiords.
> **Since** dominators are the dominant guy, he decides how we cut the pie.
> **If** I were in Tajikistan, then I would be in the Former USSR: Newly Independent States.

Although Mr. Scalene looks like he's sailing, he's actually obtuse and that's why he's leaning.
Because Isosceles has two angles with equal degrees, it looks just like a Christmas tree.

Between the sources we have listed and Eulalie's learning songs, one could support most of the topics listed in Common Core State Standards for grades first through fifth. Our ultimate goal is to collaborate with several educator–artists and create beautifully illustrated song charts for the classroom with a coordinating CD, DVD, or MP3. As an educator, it would be convenient to have one go-to source for learning songs that support grade-level content standards.

Appendix B
Writing Matrix

WRITING MATRIX

quality adjective	noun	"ly" word	strong verb

who/which clause

prepositional phrase

www.asia.b (when, while, where, as, since, if, although, because)

Appendix C
Composition Checksheet

Composition Checksheet

- Composition is double spaced.
- Dress-Ups are underlined (one of each).
- Sentence Openers are marked in margin.
- Title is underlined.

DRESS-UPS: (middle of sentence; underlined)	I	II	III
1. Quality adjective			
2. Who/which clause			
3. Strong verb			
4. "ly" word			
5. Prepositional phrase			
6. Adverb clause (www.asia.b)			

SENTENCE OPENERS: (first word of sentence; # in margin)	I	II	III
1. Subject			
2. Prepositional phrase			
3. "ly" word			
4. "ing" word			
5. Adverb clause (www.asia.b)			
6. VSS (very short sentence, 2–5 words)			
7. "ed" word			

Appendix D
Sample Syllabus

_____ University

Texts: *The Elusive Sentence: Recovering the Rudiments of Writing (TES)*
By: Rita Eulalie Hatfield, MEd &
Leta Marie Young, MA

Teaching Writing: Structure & Style (TWSS)
By: The Institute for Excellence in Writing

Mind, Brain, & Education (MBE)
Editor: David A. Sousa, EdD

Course Number: EDU ***		Spring/Fall/Winter (Day & Time)	
January ***	February ***	March ***	April ***

Instructor:	Rita Eulalie Hatfield	*Individual meetings available by appointment.
Phone:	503-281-0474	
Email:	ritaeulalie@hotmail.com	

Course Description

The purpose of this course is threefold: to introduce a sentence-level writing intervention that explicitly teaches the mechanics of crafting well-written sentences and paragraphs, to update our pedagogy for writing skills acquisition, and to provide a rationale, coupled with guided practice, for implementing a cognitively differentiated writing model. By the end of this course educators will have the tools necessary to be able to teach writing with confidence, as well as have a variety of strategies for creating lessons that accommodate for the neurodiversity of learners.

Mission Statement for _____ University

****

College of Education Mission Statement

****

Course Goal

This sentence-level writing intervention provides a hands-on concrete visual method for teaching the rudiments of writing. It eliminates the huge question in many teachers' minds that asks, "How do I teach writing?" It eliminates the huge question in students' minds that asks, "How do I fill this blank page?" The goal of this intervention is to give educators a method for writing instruction that removes the ambiguity we have all experienced as we have tried to figure out what it means to write well.

This writing model provides a systematic pedagogy for teaching writing that follows a logical progression for skills acquisition similar to how we teach music. It also teaches educators how to create lesson plans that take advantage of several special memory effects, well known in neuroscience and cognitive psychology, and uses the writing workshop as an economical opportunity to enhance learning for other content areas that so often get overlooked with today's emphasis on literacy and math. The goal of this writing intervention is to give educators a method for teaching writing that clearly defines structure and style at the sentence level and to teach educators how to implement a cognitively differentiated writing model based on the foundations of best practice.

Course Objectives and Performance Indicators

Upon completion of this course, students will be able to:

1. Understand sentential propositions, phrases, and clauses, and know how they can be manipulated to create a variety of syntactical structure and style.

    P.I. Students will create a paragraph of propositions, and a summary paragraph from a "read aloud."

    P.I. Students will create a Key Word Outline from the summary paragraph.

    P.I. Students will create a writing matrix.

    P.I. Students will summarize a narrative applying a rubric for six Dress-Ups and ten Sentence Openers.

    P.I. Students will create a song, chant, rap, or poem with movement if appropriate to support content learning for his or her summary propositions.

    P.I. Students will find an art project that supports his or her summary propositions to share with the class.

2. Analyze, evaluate, and write a report on an article from a professional journal on arts-integrated, brain-based, multimodal learning.

    P.I. Students will summarize a reference from *Mind, Brain, & Education,* and write a one to two page report using writing rubric (TWSS, 2015, p. 171).

    P.I. Students will research two articles from educational neuroscience on the value of arts-integrated learning and summarize a reference in a one to two page report using writing rubric (TWSS, 2015, p. 171). (These should relate to the article chosen from *Mind, Brain, & Education.*)

    P.I. Students will write a multiple topic research paper and scholarly analysis related to brain-based, arts-integrated learning six to eight pages in length, using "A Process Model of Unit VI" and the "Checksheet for Three-Paragraph Compositions" (TWSS, 2015, p. 107).

3. Apply knowledge of method for teaching the sentence-level writing intervention using a cognitively differentiated writing model.

   P.I. Students will create a lesson plan and describe their language and content objectives.

   P.I. Students will teach with a partner the method for sentence-level writing intervention on a topic and grade level of choice.

   P.I. Partners will create or find a song, chant, rap, or poem with movement that support their topic propositions, and share with the class.

   P.I. Partners will create and describe an arts-integrated project or activity to support their topic propositions, and demonstrate knowledge for different dispositions of knowing and learning.

   P.I. Partners will find and post for the class three arts-based websites that support their topic propositions.

   P.I. Partners will demonstrate proficiency in teaching a sentence-level writing intervention using a cognitively differentiated writing model based on a graded rubric for what success looks like.

4. Integrate elements of a writing rubric for writing from pictures.

   P.I. Students will write from a series of pictures, applying the models for key word outlining (TWSS, 2015, pp. 79 & 80).

   P.I. Students will read their compositions to the class.

5. Integrate elements of writing rubrics for creative writing.

   P.I. Students will write a five-paragraph creative composition on a topic of choice. Must include an introductory paragraph, three topics, and a concluding paragraph following the writing rubrics "Practicum Outline for Unit VII" (TWSS, 2015, pp. 140 & 145).

6. Integrate elements of writing rubrics for the Basic Essay.

P.I. Students will write a Basic Essay using their multiple topic research paper, adding an introduction and concluding paragraph following "The Essay Model" (TWSS, 2015, p. 130).

Integrate elements of writing rubric for the Super Essay.

7. P.I. Students will write a super essay using their Basic Essay, adding a Super-Introduction, Essay II (How will the research in your Basic Essay affect how you teach), Intro for Essay II, Conclusion for Essay II, and your Super-Conclusion following the "The Super-Essay Model" and "Checksheet for Five or More Paragraph Essay" (TWSS, 2015, pp. 133–36).

8. Integrate elements of writing rubric for writing Critiques.

P.I. Students will write a Critique of an article of their choice from *Mind, Brain, & Education* following the "The Critique Model" (TWSS, 2015, pp. 149 & 150).

Weekly Schedule

Date	In Class	Assignment Due Next Class
	Introductions Introduce Sentence-Level Writing Intervention • Read Aloud "Turtles" • Summary Paragraph (SP) • Key Word Outlining (KWO) • Retell (RT) from KWO • Dress-Ups (DU) • Shared Write with Dress-Ups Class Write, "The Effect of Music on Plants" • KWO & DU	**Read:** *The Elusive Sentence* (TES), pp. 1–40 **Write:** 1 page journal response on (TES) **Read:** *Teaching Writing: Structure & Style* (TWSS), Units I & II, pp. 1–30 **Write:** From handout "Vulture Bees," create a KWO, and write a summary using all six dress-ups
	Students share "Vulture Bee" write • Introduce Sentence Openers (SO) • Phrase and Clause Manipulation • Writing Matrix (WM) • Read Aloud "Rattlesnakes" Class Write, "Rattlesnakes" • KWO, RT, WM, DU, & SO Class Write, "Beluga Whales" • KWO, RT, WM Handout, "Mysterious Chameleon" Select a Partner for "Partner Teach"	**Read:** TES, pp. 41–78 **Write:** 1 page journal response on TES **Write:** Finish "Beluga Whales" **Write:** "Mysterious Chameleon" • KWO, WM, DU, SO **Read:** TWSS, Unit IV, pp. 31–64 **Write:** "Fox and the Crow" p. 28 • KWO, WM, DU, SO

Date	In Class	Assignment Due Next Class
	Students share a write • Introduce Title, Topic, & Clincher Must Relate (TT&CL) • Introduce Decorations (DC) • Introduce Summarizing a Narrative • Read Aloud "Alligators" Class Write, "Alligators" • KWO, RT, WM, DU, SO, TT&CL, DC Introduce Arts-Integrated Learning • Song, "Reptiles & Amphibians" Partner Write, "The Bat & the Nightingale" • KWO, WM	**Read:** TES, pp. 80–102 **Write:** 1 page journal response on TES **Write:** Finish "The Bat and the Nightingale" • DU, SO, TT&CL **Write:** "The Lion and the Shepherd" • KWO, WM, DU, SO, TT&CL **Read:** TWSS, Unit VI, pp. 83–108 **Read:** Select a chapter/topic from *Mind, Brain, & Education* (MBE) that interests you and read it **Write:** Create a list of propositions from chapter selected
	Students share a write • Introduce Summarizing References & Library Research Reports Class Write, "Bats" • 3 Paragraph Research Report • KWO, WM, DU, SO, TT&CL, DC • Song, "B-B-B-Bats" Partner Write 3 Paragraph Research Report • Partners Choose a Topic from Selection Provided • KWO, WM, DU, SO, TT&CL, DC	**Read:** TES, pp. 103–114 **Write:** 1 page journal response on TES **Write:** Finish Partner Write selection **Write:** 3 paragraph research report on chapter selection from MBE. • KWO, DU, SO, TT&CL, DC **Read:** TWSS, Unit V, pp. 65–82 **Write:** "Chick Model for Unit V" • KWO, DU, SO, TT&CL, DC
	Students Share Partner Write or Chick Write • Introduce Writing from Pictures Partner Write from a Selection of Pictures • KWO, WM, DU, SO, TT&CL, DC Partners Share Write with Class Partners Work on "Partner Teach"	**Read:** TES, pp. 115–123 **Write:** 1 page journal response on TES **Read:** Find and read an article from a scholarly journal related to the chapter/topic you selected from MBE. **Write:** 3 paragraph research report on the article • KWO, DU, SO, TT&CL, DC **Read:** TWSS, Unit VII, pp. 109–124 **Think:** Decide on a topic for creative writing
	Students share a write • Introduce Creative Writing—Introduction, 3 Themes, Conclusion • Introduction Gives Background, Time, Place; States 3 Themes. • Conclusion restates the 3 themes and tells which is most important	**Read:** MBE, pp. 1–40 **Write:** 1 page journal response for Chapters 1 & 2 **Read:** Find an article from a scholarly journal related to the chapter/topic you selected from MBE **Write:** 3 paragraph research report on the article

Sample Syllabus

Date	In Class	Assignment Due Next Class
	Independent Creative Write • KWO, DU, SO, TT&CL, DC Students share creative writing	• KWO, DU, SO, TT&CL, DC **Read:** TWSS, Unit VIII, pp. 125–146
	Introduce Essay Writing • Introduction & Conclusion Partner Teach Prep	**Read:** MBE, pp. 44–65 **Write:** 1 page journal response for Chapter 3 **Write:** Introduction & Conclusion for the research report from MBE & 2 articles. Fuse into a cohesive essay
	Partner Teach Partner Teach	**Read:** MBE, pp. 68–82 **Write:** 3 paragraph persuasive essay on pro & cons "Does emotion have a role in the classroom?" TWSS, pp. 140–141 **Read:** TWSS, Unit IX, Critiques, pp. 147–157
	Partner Teach Partner Teach	**Read:** MBE, pp. 84–103 **Write:** Critique Chapter 5 **Write:** Critique for chapter of choice from MBE
	Partner Teach Partner Teach	**Read:** MBE, pp. 112–129 **Write:** Critique Chapter 6 **Write:** Start Essay II as part of your Super-Essay. For Essay II think of three ways that you may implement art-integrated learning in your classroom. List your three topic ideas and turn in a KWO for each topic
	Partner Teach Partner Teach	**Read:** MBE, pp. 138–153 **Write:** Critique Chapter 7
	Partner Teach Partner Teach	**Read:** MBE, pp. 163–221 **Write:** 1 page journal response for Chapters 8, 9, 10 **Write:** Work on Super Essay
	Partner Teach Partner Teach	**Read:** MBE, pp. 227–244 **Write:** Critique Chapter 11 • KWO, DU, SO, TT&CL **Write:** Work on Super Essay
	Partner Teach Partner Teach	**Read:** MBE, pp. 249–266 **Write:** Critique Chapter 12 • KWO, DU, SO, TT&CL **Write:** Super Essay Due

Date	In Class	Assignment Due Next Class
	Partner Teach Partner Teach Final Super-Essay Due	

Appendix E
Webster's Formulas and Chants for Written Communication

Dr. Webster (1994) believed that if one wants students to permanently retain core content ideas, then one should incorporate a few mnemonic strategies like visuals, outlines, graphics, and role-play. He created nine formulas for written communication, which Eulalie has put to chant. Using an imaginary character he called "Mad Max, the demented scientist," Webster would have students take turns impersonating the character Mad Max, who uses the formulas and chants to drill his apprentices on basic writing mechanics and procedures.

The formulas are written on poster board, and the chant is printed on the back. Therefore, whoever plays Mad Max can hold up the formula for the class to see, while "Max" can read and lead the chant. Repetition promotes retention; therefore, creating a comedic routine that can be practiced a couple of times a week helps facilitate long-term memory of key content ideas. The following relates Webster's (1994) formulas for written communication:

Mad Max's Formulas & Chants
$$S => [\text{ Sub + Vrb + Obj }] + [\text{ Cap + Pun (., ?, !)}]$$

Mechanics Formula:

>1stWoP   +   MESSY = GOOD   +   .C   +   DOUBLE   +   < 100 = NUMBERS
>Indent!   > 99 = WORDS
                                                    SPACE!

                            NO REPEAT

Chant:
Indent the **first word of** a **paragraph, messy is good** (in a rough draft)
A **period** is followed by a **capital, Double space! Double space!**—so you can edit your work
Use a **number** for a number of **100 or more**, for **ninety-nine and less**; then use a **word**
In your sentence, **don't repeat a word**—follow the signs of a writing expert

Sentence Formula:
S => [Sub + Vrb + Obj] + [Cap + Pun (., ?, !)]

Chant:
If you want to write a **sentence,** let me tell you what to do—
You need a **subject, verb,** and **object,** too
Always start your sentence with a **capital**—
And end with **punctuation,** like a **period**—a **question mark**—or **exclamation point.**

Paragraph Formula:
P => 3S [tS + <2D + Clr]

Chant:
If you want to write a **paragraph,** let me tell you what to do—
You'll need more than **three sentences** to communicate ideas
Start with a **topic** sentence, then add **more than two details**
And conclude with a **clincher**—and restate your main idea

Clincher Formulas:
Paragraph Clincher: Final Clincher:
PClr => rst (mi) t   FClr => [t + Clr + T] = MUST RELATE!

Chant:
For a **paragraph clincher,** let me tell you what to do—
You **restate** the **main idea** from the topic that you choose
For a **final clincher**—three things must equate—
The **topic**—the **clincher**—and the **title**—**MUST RELATE!**

Writing Narratives (Story Sequencing Chart)

Advanced Narrative Formula:

Characters & Setting

Who:	is in the story?
Where:	does he live?
	does he go?
What:	does he look like?
	does he say?
	does he do?
When:	does it happen?

I. Who—When—Where?
II. What?
III. Problem/Solution
IV. Clincher

Problem or Surprise

What:	do they need?
	do they think?
	do they say?
	do they do?

Climax and Resolution

How:	is the problem solved?
What:	do they see/do/think/say?
	happens after?
	is learned?

Closing Clincher
(Ingham Model, 2004, p. 154)

Chant:
If you want to write a story, here's what you need to know—
Tell **who** is in the story, **where** he lives, and where he goes.
What does he look like and **what** does he say?
What does he do in a particular way?
Next you state the **problem** or relate the **surprise**
Then solve the problem; use a **clincher** for concluding—
Which means repeat the title and create a clever ending.

Finding References Formula:
Ref =>   Lk   => find + Lk + write
       Cont + Indx   t   3theme   3KWO (<2d)

Chant:
If you want to find a **reference,** let me tell you what to do—
You gotta **look** in the **contents** and the **index,** too
When you **find** a **topic,** then **look** for **three** themes
Write three key word outlines, giving **details** for each theme

Research Report Formula:
RR => Lk => Lk + Lk + write => Fuse9KWO + write => RR
    Lb + Wb   3source 3theme   9KWO   =3KWO

Chant:
For a **research report,** here's how to begin
Look in the **library** or look on the **Web**
Look for **three** sources, then **look** for **three themes**
Write nine Key Word Outlines, giving details for each theme
Fuse nine Key Word Outlines, making one for each theme
Then **write it up** and you will have the **research report** you seek.

Introductory Paragraph Formula:
IP =>   bg + tm + pl +   intro + PClr
         info   3theme

Chant:
When you need an **introductory paragraph,** like for essays and reports
Give the **background information** including **time and place**
Then introduce your **three themes** as succinctly as you can
Conclude with a **clincher** and restate your main idea.

Concluding Paragraph Formula:
CP =>   rst   =>   tell/which   +   FClr
         3themes   <import/why

Chant:
When you need a **concluding paragraph,** like for essays and reports
Restate your **three themes, telling which** is **most important**
Give your reasons **why,** then your **final clincher** state
Remember your **topic,** your **clincher,** and your **title—MUST RELATE!**

References

Abbott, M. (2001, Spring). Using music to promote L2 learning among adult learners. *TESOL Journal, 11*(1), 10–17.

Adams, M. J., & Bruck, M. (1995). Resolving the "great debate." *American Educator 19*(2), 10–20.

Anderson, J. R. & Reder, L. M. (1979). An elaborative processing explanation of depth of processing. In L. S. Cermak & F. I. M. Craik (Eds.), *Levels of Processing in Human Memory* (385–403). Hillsdale, NJ: Lawrence Erlbaum Associates.

Armstrong, T. (2000). *Multiple intelligences in the classroom.* Alexandria, VA: ASCD.

Arnosky, J. (2008). *All about turtles.* New York: Scholastic.

Auble, P. M., & Franks, J. J. (1978). The effects of effort toward comprehension on recall. *Memory & Cognition, 6*(1), 20–25.

Auble, P. M., Franks, J. J., & Soraci, Jr., S. A. (1979). Effort toward comprehension: Elaboration or "aha!"? *Memory & Cognition, 7*(6), 426–434.

Ayotte, S. (2004). The acquisition of verb forms through song (Doctoral dissertation). Retrieved from Dissertation Abstracts International (65 3356A).

Baddeley, A. D. (1990). *Human memory: Theory and practice.* Needham Heights, MA: Allyn and Bacon.

Bartlett, J. C. & Snelus, P. (1980). Lifespan memory for popular songs. *American Journal of Psychology, 93*(3), 551–560.

Bertsch, S., Pesta, B. J., Wiscott, R., & McDaniel, M. A. (2007). The generation effect: A meta-analytic review. *Memory & Cognition, 35*(2), 201–210.

Brechtel, M. (2001). *Bringing it all together: Language and literacy in the multilingual classroom.* Carlsbad, CA: Dominie Press.

Brooks, D. (2011). *The social animal.* New York, NY: Random House.

Brown, R. & Kulik, J. (1977). Flashbulb memories. *Memory & Cognition, 5*(1), 73–99.

Brown, S., Martinez, M. J., & Parsons, L. M. (2006). Music and language side by side in the brain: A PET study of the generation of melodies and sentence. *European Journal of Neuroscience, 23,* 2791–2803.

Bruner, J. S. (1961). The act of discovery. *Harvard Education Review, 31*(1), 21–32.

Burnaford, G., Brown, S., Doherty, J., & McLaughlin, H. J. (2007). *Arts integration frameworks, research, & practice: A literature review.* Arts Education Partnership.

Burns, M. S., Griffen, P., & Snow, C. E. (1998). *Preventing reading difficulties in young children.* Washington, DC: National Academic Press.

Burnstein, J. H., & Knotts, G. (2010). Creating connections: Integrating the visual arts with social studies. *Social Studies and the Young Learners, 23*(1), 20–23.

Cade, T., & Gunter, P. (2002, May). Teaching students with severe emotional or behavioral disorders to use a musical mnemonic technique to solve basic division calculations. *Behavioral Disorders, 27*(3), 208–214.

Cahill, L., & McGaugh, J. L. (1995), A novel demonstration of enhanced memory associated with emotional arousal. *Consciousness and Cognition, 4,* 410–421.

Cambourne, B. (1998). *Cambourne's seven conditions of learning.* Retrieved March 5, 2009, from http://faculty.nipissingu.ca/hancym/powerpoints/Lesson1-Cambournes_Seven_Conditions_of_Learning.

Campabello, N., De Carlo, M. J., O'Neil, J., & Vacek, M. J. (2002). *Music enhances learning.* Chicago, IL: Action Research Project. Saint Xavier University.

Campion, D. (2011). Hong Kong higher ed embracing the liberal arts. *The Sunday Oregonian,* September 25, B7.

Catterall, J. S., & Waldorf, F. (1999). Chicago arts partnerships in education: Evaluation summary. In E. Fiske (ed.), *Champion of change: The impact of the arts on learning.* Washington, DC: The Arts Education Partnership and the President's Committee on the Arts and Humanities.

Cavanagh, S. (2003). Oregon study outlines standards for college preparedness. *Education Week, 22*(25), 6.

Cognition. (2011). *Oxford Dictionaries.* Retrieved February 11, 2011 from http://www.oxforddictionaries.com/us/definition/american_english/cognition.

Cohen, R. L. (1983). The effect of encoding variables on the free recall of words and action events. *Memory & Cognition, 11,* 575–582.

Conner, J. E. (1982). Half a mind a terrible thing to waste. *For Adults Only, 15*(4), 422–426.

Conrad, J. (1990). *Heart of darkness.* New York : Dover Publications, Inc.

Cook, R. J. (1958). *One hundred and one famous poems.* Chicago, IL: Contemporary Books.

Craik, F. I. M., & Lockhart, R. S. (1972). Levels of processing: A framework for memory research. *Journal of Verbal Learning and Verbal Behavior, 11,* 671–684.

Craik, F. I. M., & Watkins, M. J. (1973). The role of rehearsal in short-term memory. *Journal of Verbal Learning and Verbal Behavior, 12*(6), 599–607.

Crowder, R. G., Serafine, M. L., & Repp, B. (1990). Physical interaction and association by contiguity in memory for the words and melodies of songs. *Memory & Cognition, 18*(5), 469–476.

Culham, R. (2005). *6 + 1 traits of writing.* New York: Scholastic, Inc.

Defeyter, M. A., Russo, R., & McPartlin, P. L. (2009). The picture superiority effect in recognition memory: A developmental study using the response signal procedure. *Cognitive Development, 24*(3), 265–273.

Dennison, P. E. (2006). *Brain gym and me.* Ventura, CA: Edu-Kinesthetics.

Deutsch, D. (2010, July/August). Speaking in tones: Music and language are partners in the brain. *Scientific American.* Retrieved July 19, 2010, from http://www.scientificamerican.com/article/speaking-in-tones-jul10/.

Dewey, J. (1902). *The child and the curriculum.* Chicago, IL: University of Chicago Press.

Efland, A. D. (2002). *Art and cognition: Integrating the visual arts in the curriculum.* New York: Teachers College Press.

Eisner, E. W. (2002). The kind of schools we need. *Phi Delta Kappa, 83*(8), 578–83.

Fedewa, A. L., & Ahn, S. (2011). The effects of physical activity and physical fitness on children's achievement and cognitive outcomes: A meta-analysis. *Research Quarterly For Exercise and Sport, 82*(3).

Fountas, I. C., & Pinnell G. S. (2001). *Guiding readers and writers: Teaching comprehension genre, and content literacy.* Portsmouth, NH: Heinemann.

Fulkerson, R. (2001). Of pre- and post-process: Reviews and ruminations. *Composition Studies, 29*(2), 93–119.

Gardner, H. (1999). *Intelligence reframed.* New York: Basic Books.

Garner, A. M. (2009). Singing and moving: Teaching strategies for audiation in children. *Music Educators Journal, 95*(4), 1–6.

Gazzaniga, M. (2008). *Learning arts, and the brain: The Dana Consortium report on arts and cognition.* New York: Dana Press.

Gfeller, K. E. (1983). Musical mnemonics as an aid to retention with normal and learning disabled students. *The Journal of Music, 20,* 179–189.

Ginns, P. (2005). Meta-analysis of the modality effect. *Learning and Instruction, 4,* 313–331.

Glasser, W. (1975). *Schools without failure.* New York: Harper & Row.

Goll, P. S. (2004, Winter). Mnemonic strategies creating schemata for learning enhancement. *Education, 125*(2), 306–312.

Goodman, N. (1978). *Languages of art.* Indianapolis, IN: Hackett.

Gordon, E. E. (2003). *Learning sequences in music.* Chicago: GIA Publications.

Griffen, P., Snow, C. C., & Burns, M. S. (1998). *Preventing reading difficulties in young children.* Washington, DC: National Academy Press.

Gullatt, D. E. (2007). Research links the arts with student academic gains. *The Education Forum, 71*(3), 211–220.

Hardiman, M. M. (2003). *Connecting brain research with effective teaching: The brain-targeted teaching model.* Lanham, MD: Rowman & Littlefield Publishers.

Hardiman, M. M. (2010). The creative-artistic brain. In D. A. Sousa (Eds.), *Mind, brain, & education: Neuroscience implications for the classroom.* (chap. 11, pp. 226–246) Bloomington, IN: Solution Tree Press.

Harvey, S., & Goudvis, A. (2007). *Strategies that work.* Portland, ME: Stenhouse.

Hikari, K., & Snodgrass, J. G. (2000). Does the generation effect occur for pictures? *The American Journal of Psychology, 113*(1), 95–121.

Ho, W., & Law, W. (2004). Values, music, and education in China. *Music Education Research, 6*(2), 149–167.

Hodges, D. (1982). A teacher's guide to memory techniques. *Focus on Productivity, 7,* 23–27.

Hodges, D. A. (2000, September). Implications of music and brain research. *Music Educators Journal, 87*(2), 17–22.

Huitt, W., & Hummel, J. (2003). Piaget's theory of cognitive development. *Educational Psychology Interactive.* Retrieved 2/21/2011 from http://www.edpsyc interactive.org/topics/cognition/piaget.html.

Ingham, A. G. (2004). *The blended sound-sight program of learning.* Nisku, Alberta: Nisku Printers.

Jacoby, L. L. (1978). On interpreting the effects of repetition: Solving a problem verses remembering a solution. *Journal of Verbal Learning and Behavior, 17,* 649–667.

Jefferies, K. J., Fritz, J. B., & Braun, A. R. (2003). An H2150 PET study of brain activation during singing and speaking. *Neuroreport, 14*(5), 749–754.

Jensen, E. (2000). *Music with the brain in mind.* Thousand Oaks, CA: Corwin Press.

Jensen, E. (2005). *Teaching with the brain in mind.* Alexandria, VA: ASCD.

Johansson, B. B. (2008). Language and music: What do they have in common and how do they differ? A neuroscientific approach. *European Review, 16*(4), 413–427.

Jones, R. (1995). Writing wrongs. *Executive Educator, 17(*April*),* 18–24.

Kantz, A. (2004). *Sing to greet the world around me.* Retrieved from www .precisionsongs.com.

Kawagley, A. O. (2006). *A Yupiaq worldview: A pathway to ecology and spirit.* Long Grove, IL: Waveland Press.

Keene, E. O., & Zimmermann, S. (2007). *Mosaic of thought.* Portsmouth, NH: Heinemann.

Kensinger, E. A., & Schacter, D. L. (2008). Memory and emotion. In M. Lewis, J. M. Haviland-Jones, & L. Feldman Barrett (Eds.), *Handbook of emotions* (601–617). New York: Guilford.

Kilgour, A. R., Jakobson, L. S., & Cuddy, L. L. (2000). Music training rate of presentation as mediators of text and song recall. *Memory & Cognition, 28*(5), 700–710.

Kim, B. (2001). Social constructivism. In M. Orey (Ed.), Emerging perspectives on learning, teaching, and technology. Retrieved February 27, 2011, from http://projects.coe.uga.edu/epitt/indes.php?title=Social_Constructivism.

Kimball, K. (2010). Engaging auditory modalities through the use of music in information literacy instruction. *Reference & User Services Quarterly, 49,* 316–319.

Kinjo, H., & Snodgrass, J. G. (2000). Does the generation effect occur for pictures? *The American Journal of Psychology, 113*(1), 95–121.

Klein, S. B., & Kihlstrom, J. F. (1986). Elaboration, organization, and the self-reference effect in memory. *Journal of Experimental Psychology, 115*(1), 26–38.

Kolb, K. A. (1985). *The learning style inventory.* Boston: McBee & Company.

Kong, A., & Peterson, D. P. (2003). The road to participation: The construction of literacy practice in a learning community of linguistically diverse learners. *Research in the Teaching of English, 38*(1), 85–124.

Krashen, S. D. (1992). *Fundamentals of language education.* Chicago: McGraw Hill.
Krashen, S. D. (2003). *Explorations in language acquisition and use.* Portsmouth, NH: Heinemann.
Landon, B. (2008). *Building great sentences: Exploring the writer's craft.* Chantilly, VA: The Teaching Company.
Lasagna, L. (1964). *Hippocratic oath, modern version.* Retrieved February 11, 2011 from http://guides.library.jhu.edu/c.php?g=202502&p=1335759.
Lemov, D. (2010). *Teach like a champion.* San Francisco: Jossey-Bass.
Levin, M. E., & Levin, J. R. (1990). Scientific mnemonics: Methods for maximizing more memory. *American Education Research, 27*(2), 301–321.
Li, X., & Brand, M. (2009). Effectiveness of music on vocabulary acquisition language usage and meaning for mainland Chinese ESL learners. *Contributions to Music Education 36*(1), 73–84.
MacLeod, C. M., Gopie, N., Hourihan, K. L., Neary, K. R., & Ozubko, J. D. (2010). The production effect: Delineation of a phenomenon. *Journal of Experimental Psychology, 36*(3), 671–685.
Maess, B., & Koelsch, S. (2001). Musical syntax is processed in Broca's area: An MEG study. *Nature Neuroscience, 4,* 540–545.
Mandell, J., & Wolf, J. (2003). *Acting, learning, and change.* Portsmouth, NH: Heinemann.
Mastropieri, M. A., Sweda, J., & Scruggs, T. E. (2000). Putting mnemonic strategies to work in an inclusive classroom. *Learning Disabilities Research & Practice, 15*(2), 69–74.
McCarthy, B. (1986). *The hemispheric mode indicator.* Barrington, IL: Excel.
McCarthy, B. (1987). *The 4MAT system.* Barrington, IL: Excel.
McCarthy, B. (1997). A tale of four learners: 4MAT. *Educational Leadership, 54*(6), 46–51.
McDaniel, M. A., & Bugg, J. M. (2008). Instability in memory phenomena: A common puzzle and unifying explanation. *Psychonomic Bulletin & Review, 15*(2), 237–255.
McGaugh, J. L. (2004). The amygdala modulates the consolidation of memories of emotionally arousing experiences. *Annual Review of Neuroscience, 27*(1), 1–28.
McNeil, M. (2011). A new year brings a new reality for Oregon's Public Schools: Changes. In Haight, *Today's OEA, 86*(1), 16–21.
Melnick, S. A., Witmer, J. T., & Strickland, M. J. (2011). Cognition and student learning through the arts. *Arts Education Policy Review, 12*(3), 154–162.
Mintzer, M. Z., & Snodgrass, J. G. (1999). The picture superiority effect: Support for the distinctiveness model. *American Journal of Psychology, 112*(1), 113–146.
Mohr, G., Engelkamp, J., & Zimmer, H. D. (1989). Recall and recognition of self-performed acts. *Psychological Research, 51*(4), 181–187.
Mora, C. F. (2000). Foreign language acquisition and melody singing. *ELT Journal, 54*(2), 146–153.
Morrongiello, B. A., & Roes, C. L. (1990). Children's memory for new songs: Integration or independent storage of words and tunes. *Journal of Experimental Child Psychology, 50*(1), 25–38.

National Reading Panel. (2000). *Report of the national reading panel: Teaching children to read: An evidence-based assessment of the scientific research literature on reading and its implications on reading instruction.* Washington, DC: US Government Printing Office, NIH Publication No. 00-4769. Retrieved from http://www.nichd.nih.gov/research/supported/Pages/nrp.aspx/publications/summary.htm.

Noll, J. W. (2011). *Taking sides: Clashing views on educational issues.* New York: McGraw-Hill.

Olsen, K. D. (1995). *Synergy: Transforming America's high schools through integrated thematic instruction.* Kent, WA: Susan Kovalik & Associates.

Ozubko, J. D., & MacLeod, C. M. (2010). The production effect in memory: Evidence that distinctiveness underlies the benefit. *Journal of Experimental Psychology, 36*(6), 1543–1547.

Paquette, K. R., & Rieg, S. A. (2008). Using music to support literacy development of young English language learners. *Early Education Journal, 37*(3), 227–232. DOI: 10.1007/s10643-0277-9.

Parsons, M. (1992). Cognition as interpretation in art education. In B. Reimer & R. A. Smith (Eds.). *The arts, education, and aesthetic knowing: Ninety-first yearbook of the National Society for the Study of Education* (Part II, 70–91). Chicago: University of Chicago Press.

Patel, A. D. (2003). Language, music, syntax, and the brain. *Nature Neuroscience, 6,* 674–681.

Peregoy, S. F., & Boyle, O.F. (2008). *Reading, writing, and learning in ESL.* Boston: Pearson Education.

Peretz, I. (2006). The nature of music from a biological perspective. *Cognition, 100*(1), 1–32.

Peretz, I., Gagnon, L., Hebert, L., & Macoir, J. (2004). Singing in the brain: Insights from cognitive neuropsychology. *Music Perception, 21*(3), 373–390.

Peretz, I., Radeau, M., & Arguin, M. (2004). Two-way interactions between music and language: Evidence from priming recognition of tune and lyrics in familiar songs. *Memory & Cognition, 32*(1), 142–152.

Peynircioglu, Z. F., Rabinovitz, B. E., & Tompson, J. L. W. (2008). Memory and metamemory for songs: The relative effectiveness of titles, lyrics, and melodies as cues for each other. *Psychology of Music, 36*(1), 47–61.

Piaget, J., & Inhedler, B. (1969). *The psychology of the child.* New York: Basic Books.

Pink, D. H. (2006). *A whole new mind: Why right-brainers will rule the future.* New York: Riverhead Books.

Podlozny, A. (2000). Strengthening verbal skills through the use of classroom drama: A clear link. *Journal of Aesthetic Education, 34*(3/4), 239–275.

Pudewa, A. (2004). *Nurturing competent communicators.* Tacoma, WA: IEW.

Pudewa, A. (2015). *Teaching writing: Structure and style.* Locust Grove, OK: The Institute for Excellence in Writing.

Rainey, D. W., & Larsen, J. D. (2002, Winter). The effect of familiar melodies on initial learning and long-term memory for unconnected text. *Music Perception, 20*(2), 173–186.

Reder, L. M. (1979). The role of elaboration in memory for prose. *Cognitive Psychology, 11*(2), 221–234.

Rinne, L., Gregory, E., Yarmolinskaya, J., & Hardiman, M. (2011). Why arts integration improves long-term retention of content. *Mind, Brain, and Education, 5*(2), 89–96.

Root-Bernstein, R. (2005). Roger Sperry: Ambicerebral man. *Leonardo, 38*(3), 224–225.

Rundus, D. (1971). Analysis of rehearsal processes in free recall. *Journal of Experimental Psychology, 89*(1), 63–77.

Sacks, O. (2007). *Musicophilia: Tales of music and the brain.* New York: Vintage Books.

Saddler, B. (2007). Best practices in teaching sentence construction skills. In S. Graham, C. MacArthur, & J. Fitzgerald (Eds.), *Best practices in writing instruction* (163–178). New York: Guilford.

Saddler, B., & Asaro-Saddler, K. (2010). Writing better sentences: Sentence-combining instruction in the classroom. *Preventing School Failure, 54*(3), 159–163.

Samson, S., & Zatorre, R. J. (1991). Recognition of memory for text and melody of songs after unilateral temporal lobe lesion: Evidence for dual encoding. *Learning, Memory, & Cognition, 17*(4), 793–804.

Schmoker, M. (2006). *Results now.* Alexandria, VA: ASCD.

Schoepp, K. (2001). Reasons for using songs in the ESL/EFL classroom. *The Internet TESL Journal, 72.* Retrieved from http://iteslj.org/Articles/Schoepp-Songs.html.

Scruggs, T. E., & Mastropieri, M. A. (2000). The effectiveness of mnemonic instruction for students with learning and behavior problems; An update research synthesis. *Journal of Behavioral Education, 10*(2/3), 163–173.

Selfe, C. L. (2009). The movement of air, the breath of meaning: Aurality and multimodal composing. *CCC 60*(4), 616–663.

Selkrig, M., & Bottrell, C. (2009). Transformative learning for pre-service teachers: When too much art education is barely enough. *The International Journal of Learning, 16*(1), 395–408.

Shepard, R. N. (1967). Recognition memory for words, sentences, and pictures. *Journal of Verbal Learning and Verbal Behavior, 6*(1), 156–163.

Slamecka, N. J., & Graf, P. (1978). The generation effect: Delineation of a phenomenon. *Journal of Experimental Psychology: Human Learning and Memory, 4*(6), 592–604.

Smithrim, K., & Upitis, R. (2005). Learning through the arts: Lessons of engagement. *Canadian Journal of Education, 28*(1/2), 109–127.

Sousa, D. A. (2007). *How the special needs brain learns.* Thousand Oaks, CA: Corwin.

Sousa, D. A. (2010). How science met pedagogy. In D. A. Sousa (Eds.), *Mind, brain, & education: Neuroscience implications for the classroom* (chap. 1, 8–24). Bloomington, IN: Solution Tree Press.

Sousa, D. A. (2011a). *How the brain learns.* Thousand Oaks, CA: Corwin.

Sousa, D. A. (2011b). *How the ELL brain learns.* Thousand Oaks, CA: Corwin.

Sperry, R. W. (1973). Lateral specialization of cerebra function in the surgically separated hemispheres. In F. J. McGuigan & R. A. Schoonover (Eds.). *The psychology of thinking studies of covert processes* (chap. 6, 209–229). New York: Academic Press.

Sperry, R. W. (1982). Nobel lecture: Some effects of disconnecting the cerebral hemispheres. *Science, 217,* 1223–1226.

Sprenger, M. (1998). Memory lane is a two-way street. *Educational Leadership,* November.

Suzuki violin school. (2007). Los Angeles, CA: Summy-Birchard, Inc.

Thorndike & Barnhart Comprehensive Desk Dictionary. (1962). New York: Doubleday.

Toyota, H. (2010). Developmental changes in the effects of types of self-corrected elaboration on incidental memory. *Japanese Psychological Research, 52*(1), 41–47.

Tripp, R. T. (1970). *The international thesaurus of quotations.* New York: Harper & Row.

Tyre, P. (2011). *The good school: How smart parents get their kids the education they deserve.* New York: Henry Holt and Company.

Tyre, P. (2012). The writing revolution. *The Atlantic,* October, 96–101.

Tyrer, G. (2002). Whole-brain learning for literacy. *Literacy Today,* September, 8–9.

Vaughn, K. (2000). Music and mathematics: Modest support for oft-claimed relationship. *Journal of Aesthetic Education, 34* (3/4, Special Issue: The Arts and Academic Achievement: What the Evidence Shows), 149–166.

Vygotsky, L. (1929). *The problem of the cultural development of the child.* Retrieved March 5, 2011, from http://www.marxists.org/archive/vygotsky/works/1929/cultural_development.htm.

Vygotsky, L. (1934a). *The problem of the environment.* Retrieved March 5, 2011, from, http://www.marxists.org/archive/vygotsky/works/1934/environment.htm.

Vygotsky, L. (1934b/1986). *Thought and language.* Cambridge, MA: The MIT Press.

Walker, D. M. (1995). *Connecting right and left brain: Increasing academic performance of African American students through the arts.* Dallas, TX: Indiana University South Bend.

Wallace, W. T. (1994). Memory for music: Effect on recall of text. *Journal of Experimental Psychology, 20*(6), 1471–1485.

Webster, J. B. (1994). *Blended structure and style in composition.* Saskatoon, Canada: Dalhousie University.

Whitman, O., & King, E. (1953). *There's a rainbow in every teardrop.* Van Nuys, CA: Alfred.

Williams, D. L. (2010). The speaking brain. In D. A. Sousa (Eds.), *Mind, brain, & education: Neuroscience implications for the classroom* (chap. 5, 84–109). Bloomington, IN: Solution Tree Press.

Wolfe, P. (2006). Brain-compatible learning: Fad or foundation? *School Administration, 63*(11), 10–15.

Wolgemuth, J. R., Cobb, R. B., & Alwell, M. (2008). The effects of mnemonic interventions on academic outcomes for youth with disabilities: A systematic review. *Learning Disabilities Research and Practice, 23*(1), 1–10.

Wordsworth Dictionary of Musical Quotations. (1991). Compiled by Derik Watson. Ware, Hertsfordshire: Wordsworth Editions.

Yates, F. (1956). *The art of memory.* Chicago: University of Chicago Press.

Young, M. R. (2010). The art and science of fostering engaged learning. *Academy of Educational Leadership Journal, 14,* 1–18.

Zaromb, F. M., & Roediger III, H. L. (2009). The effects of "effort after meaning" on recall: Differences in within-and between-subjects designs. *Memory & Cognition, 37*(4), 447–463.

Zemelman, S., Daniels, H., & Hyde, A. (2005). *Best practice: Today's standards for teaching & learning in America's schools.* Portsmouth, NH: Heinemann.

Zike, Dinah. (1992). *Big book of books and activities.* San Antonio, TX: Dina-Might Adventures.

www.ingramcontent.com/pod-product-compliance
Lightning Source LLC
Chambersburg PA
CBHW031553300426
44111CB00006BA/295